Teachers Rock!

John Morrissey

Thanks

a collection of personal stories

Thanks
to one of my
FAVORITE
TEACHERS

John Morrissey

REACHABLE
STARS PRESS
Omaha, Nebraska

ISBN10: 0-9827211-1-0
ISBN13: 978-0-9827211-1-7
Library of Congress Control Number: 2010908971

Reachable Stars Press
P.O. Box 540851
Omaha, Nebraska 68154
www.JohnPresents.com

Book Design: Gary James Withrow
Production & Marketing: Concierge Marketing, Inc.
    www.ConciergeMarketing.com

Printed in the United States
10 9 8 7 6 5 4 3 2

To all teachers everywhere—
You have the most important job in the world.

Contents

I can live for two months
on a good compliment.

—Mark Twain

Introduction

I STARTED ASKING PEOPLE to tell me about one of their favorite teachers. Just for fun. In line at the supermarket. On an airplane. At the barber shop. I asked hundreds and hundreds. And here's what I found: everyone has a favorite teacher or two.

I've traveled across the country, and I have yet to find a person who doesn't have a favorite teacher. Not only were people willing to tell me about their favorite teachers, but their eyes lit up, a smile crossed their face, and they spoke very passionately about them. They even blurted out the teacher's name, taking no time at all for recollection (instead of thinking *now what was his or her name?*).

These stories represent a cross-section of responses from across the country—even from around the world and from all grades and types of academic institutions.

This book is my love song to the teaching profession, a profession in which I am proud to have spent my entire life. There may be equally beloved professions, but there are none greater because teachers have the chance to invest in the hearts and minds of students with experiences that can be life-changing.

Teachers have the power to create unforgettable positive experiences. Teaching is the ultimate way to affect the outcome of one's corner of the world. To positively influence a student's life is more valuable than any amount of money.

My Favorite Teacher

As I think back over my life to discover who first got me interested in teaching, I would have to say it was my Aunt Marge, who is a good representation, in many ways, of "every teacher."

Aunt Marge taught junior high English. For forty-four years. In a small town in Iowa! She was a saint.

Marge never married and never had kids of her own. Her students were her kids. She had thousands of them over the years. She loved each and every one of them, and each and every one of them loved her back. She would do anything for them. They would do anything for her. She was stern, but in a caring sort of way.

Marge's sister was my mother, Mary Agnes, who had eight kids of her own. Seven boys and one girl. Marge would visit us every Christmas, Easter, and summer. She owned a Chevy car her entire life and would sing "See the USA in your Chevrolet" as she drove down the street. She

3

always brought us bags of candy. Her favorites were lemon drops and jelly candies.

She used to tell us stories of her responsibilities when she first started teaching in 1936. She got up at 4:30 each morning to walk to the one-room schoolhouse to prepare it for the school day. During cold months, she went behind the schoolhouse to bring in wood and coal for the fireplace and pot-bellied stove to keep her students warm. She also carried in buckets of water from the well for water breaks throughout the day. Oftentimes she had to chase mice away so they wouldn't scare the children.

When I was a teenager, Aunt Marge used to bring papers home to correct over her vacation. "A teacher's job is never finished," she would say. I volunteered to help her grade the spelling papers. She knew it would not only help her out, it would help me learn to spell. She never missed an opportunity to teach. I later followed in her footsteps by becoming a teacher.

After she retired from teaching, she visited me in Los Angeles, where I was the Dean of Students at Beverly Hills Prep School. She was seventy-five years old, and it was the first time she was ever on an airplane. She wasn't interested in seeing Hollywood, Beverly Hills, or Disneyland when she came to L.A. She just wanted to see the ocean, go to a Dodgers game (she was an avid baseball fan), and go to school to help me. And she did all three. After the Dodgers game, we went to my house to grade papers.

We had come full circle—I once graded her students' school papers, now she graded my students' papers.

Aunt Marge died in 1992, at the age of seventy-nine, with no money to her name, but she was the richest person I've ever known. She was a teacher.

Who Is Your Favorite Teacher?

People forget the rich and famous (can you name the 1990 Miss America, the 2000 Best Actor Oscar winner, or the third richest person in the world?). But they do not forget those teachers who taught, inspired, encouraged, and loved them (now name three of your favorite teachers).

I invite you to reach out to your favorite teachers and let them know what they've meant to you. It is my hope that these stories inspire you to write your own story, or note, to a teacher who made a difference in your life. Or pass this book on to them. In the front of the book or in your note, simply write, "*You* are one of *my* favorite teachers."

—John Morrissey

A Spelling Test to Remember

by Lisa Pelto
about her Fifth-Grade Teacher, Mrs. Ranks

"DYNAMITE COMES IN SMALL packages," she'd say. I was the smallest in Mrs. Ranks's fifth-grade class—all of forty-eight inches tall and sixty pounds. My mother cut my hair into a pixie, somehow making me seem even tinier. Mrs. Ranks was quite short and stout, though in her day, she might have been pixie-like also. Perhaps that is why we had a special bond.

Every day, I would pull my stubbornly straight hair into a barrette and clip the straggling hairs up with a bobby pin on each side. Then I'd slip on one of my few pretty, but tattered dresses (back in the '60s in our public school district, girls were not allowed to wear slacks or jeans). I'd finish my look with a dainty white pair of socks with lace edging and shiny black shoes that were always too big because my mother would put them on layaway months ahead, guessing my future size.

Mrs. Ranks always noticed my pretty dresses and shiny shoes, even though I wore the same ones week after week. Every day, she wore a dark suit with a string of pearls and big, thick black shoes that clicked against the tile floors in the classroom. Her hair was silvery black, set in perfectly tight curls, except for the one stray lock that escaped over her ear whenever she wore her thick glasses that made her eyes look enormous.

Both Mrs. Ranks and I freely admitted that I was her pet. I was the one selected to hand out the special handwriting pens to those who had earned them for perfect penmanship. I was the one she called on to borrow one of my prized bobby pins when one of the boys had bangs so long she couldn't see his eyes. I was her go-to person for everything.

One day as I helped her clean erasers, she smiled and said, "I wish I had a daughter just like you." I loved her, and she loved me.

I also loved a boy named Kirk, and Mrs. Ranks knew it. I sat in the first row by the door, second seat from her desk, of course. Kirk sat six rows over, one seat ahead. He was beautiful with his blue eyes, dark curls, and huge white teeth that I somehow knew meant he'd be really tall someday. I stole a peek at Kirk every chance I could, and I watched and hoped one day he would just glance back at me and our eyes would meet and it would be love. I dreamed and daydreamed about that moment.

On Thursdays, we had spelling tests. Everyone took out a piece of lined paper, a pencil (or our special perfect-penmanship pens), and received our instructions the same way each week.

"Pupils," Mrs. Ranks would say from her perch behind her desk, "please write your name at the top of the paper, and number your paper down the left-hand side from 1 to 10. This is your spelling test, so no talking and no looking at your neighbor's paper."

"I will read the word, use it in a sentence, and repeat the word," she said.

I knew the routine well, and I executed it with precision and perfection week after week. As she read the words, I looked up to the right to my thinking spot, then to the left to steal a glance at Kirk as if I was really thinking hard. Then I would write the word just as I had learned it in my perfect penmanship.

During the test, Mrs. Ranks would walk slowly across the room, from end to end, back to front, watching as we wrote. She would always put her finger on my paper as she passed and give me a little wink as if to say, "You're perfect again!"

One windy day in the spring of 1969, we were preparing to take one of these fifth-grade spelling tests. The classroom door was closed, and the windows by Kirk were open, with only a slight breeze of fresh air coming in. I was in my favorite blue plaid dress with the white sailor collar accented with a big pink ribbon.

Mrs. Ranks told us to get out our paper, and then I knew I had waited a moment too long to ask for a hall pass to visit the girls' room. I would have to wait, and it would not be easy.

Mrs. Ranks read the first word from her silent letter list. "*Knowledge.* Students go to school to gain knowledge. *Knowledge.*"

She walked from the door across the front of the room. "Number two. *Answer.* When you need an answer to a question, ask for help. *Answer.*" She turned down the row next to Kirk and walked to the back of the classroom.

"Number three. *Laughter.* Laughter fills the heart with joy. *Laughter.*"

My need to visit the girls' room was becoming unbearable, so I raised my hand in a frantic wave to her, glimpsing at Kirk from the corner of my eye, hoping he wouldn't notice.

Still without acknowledging me, Mrs. Ranks said, "Number four. *Eighth.* He had his eighth piece of candy and became sick. *Eighth.*"

She slowly walked up a row in the middle, her thick shoes clicking a slow, steady rhythm that sounded like a dripping faucet. Again, I raised my hand urgently, and again I peeked at Kirk, but this time to make *sure* he was *not* looking.

In that instant, the door swung open from a huge gust of wind, my paper took flight, my dress blew up around my chest, and I tried to grab them both. Simultaneously, I felt the warmth of pee running down my legs, filling my shiny black shoes and making a pool of warm yellow embarrassment under my desk.

Horrified, I waved my hand at Mrs. Ranks again, who walked slowly to the back of the room by the sink and, without wavering, said, "Number five. *Knight.* The knight rode into the kingdom on his horse. *Knight.*"

She grabbed a pile of paper towels, walked up my row and touched my paper as usual, then dropped the towels on the floor, stepped on them, and pushed them under my desk into the pool of pee with her big black shoe—not missing a step.

"Number six. *Brighten.*" She continued, giving me a wink. I looked up to the right to my thinking spot, then over to the left just in time to see Kirk not noticing me once again. "She opened the window to brighten the room. *Brighten.*"

Mrs. Ranks gave us the tenth spelling word just before the bell rang. As everyone was finishing up and gathering their things, she said, "Lisa, can you stay for a minute and help me with the board?" I sat there while the room cleared, and together we cleaned up my mess talking about my mother's garden rather than about what happened that morning. To my knowledge, no one else ever knew, most of all Kirk.

That year, my favorite teacher taught me much more than history, math, and spelling. She taught me that it is worth it to save other people from life's little embarrassing moments, like stopping someone from walking out of the bathroom with toilet paper stuck to their shoe, or quietly signaling an open zipper, or stopping a total stranger to tell them they have spinach in their teeth.

She taught me life's greatest lessons: to always be considerate, selfless, and helpful without waving a banner to advertise it. Thank you, Mrs. Ranks! (As for Kirk, as he grew older, he did finally grow into those enormous teeth. He was beautiful and aloof all through high school. At our ten-year high school reunion, he had lost most of his hair, was divorced with three kids, and had a beer gut. I, on the other hand, looked so smoking hot, he peed *his* pants.)

Lisa Pelto continues to be a complete suck-up teacher's pet to this day. She is married to Eric, the guy dubbed "the trouble maker" at his grade school. They have two daughters. She owns a Midwestern publishing firm and serves on several volunteer boards and committees in schools and civic organizations that work with children. She has deep appreciation, respect, and love for the spirit of those who choose teaching as their life's ambition.

Standing on the Shoulders of Giants

by Ed Rush
about his Second-Grade Teacher, Sister Maureen

I GET GOOSE BUMPS when I think of this. My second-grade teacher was Sister Maureen, in a Catholic grade school outside of Philadelphia. A couple of years earlier, I had failed kindergarten (which should tell you a little bit about me). In first grade I lived in California, and my parents separated. So I moved to Philadelphia in the middle of the school year.

I was pretty much of a goof-off—not very good at school. I didn't care too much and I really didn't have much confidence in myself. So I advanced to second grade still as a goof-off kid. That's where Sister Maureen comes in.

I don't know exactly how she did it. You know how you basically meet someone's expectations? For example, if they think you're a hero and a rock star, then you're going to be, to them, a hero and a rock star. Or if they think you're stupid and meaningless, then that's what you're going to be to them too.

For some reason, Sister Maureen saw a lot in me, and she really had high expectations for me. She treated me like I was really smart, and as a result of that, I was really smart.

It's amazing, because that year, in second grade, I won the award for highest scholastic achievement, which basically means I had the highest grades in class. Now that was a big surprise to my entire family, as you might imagine. But it's so interesting that literally in one school year, nine months, I went from being a goof-off, underachieving kid to the smartest kid in class.

And nothing changed in my gray matter. I was still the same flesh and blood, still the same cells, and still the same brain that I had when I walked into that class. The only difference was the way Sister Maureen treated me and her confidence in me.

I thought, "Okay, I'll just live up to those expectations." That became my history. I always did well after that. I got into good schools, and I thank her for that.

I remember once when we did a class play, she picked me to be the lead, and that made me feel like I was an important person and that I was smart.

At the end of the school year, Sister Maureen went around to every single person in the class and told them something positive she saw in them. I actually remember sitting there thinking, "Wow, I wonder what she's going to say about so-and-so, who's a real knucklehead." But she came up with something positive to say about every single person in class.

It reminds me of a quote that I believe is attributed to Albert Einstein. To paraphrase, he said, "If I've been able to see farther, it's because I've been standing on the shoulders of giants." Sister Maureen is an example of a person who didn't have a lot of worldly possessions or children of her own, but she reached so many people. She influenced me in a way that I can now influence others.

If I saw Sister Maureen today, I would tell her exactly what I've said here. I would also give her a copy of my book, *Fighter Pilot Performance for Business,* and show her one of my presentations, and tell her "thank you!" Thank you because I'm able to positively influence other people's lives because of what she taught me and the confidence she instilled in me.

Ed Rush, current President of Ed Rush & Associates, is a former fighter pilot with the United States Marine Corps and an expert in the fields of leadership training and performance under pressure. His fast-track military career has taken him from his first flight in the FA-18 Hornet to leading combat missions over Iraq. He has piloted the T-34, T-2, A-4, F-18, UH-1N, and the FT-7. As one of the Marine Corps' top instructors, he has taught and led hundreds of the Marine Corps' select fighter pilots. This graduate of the Navy Fighter Weapons School (Top Gun) has spoken before thousands and is regarded as an expert in leadership training, instructing, and presenting. Rush can be found at www.EdRush.com.

Fear Factor

by Evonne Williams
about her Fifth- and Sixth-Grade Teacher, Dixie Raatz

TERRIFIED. THERE WAS NO other way to describe it. Every child's fear of entering fifth grade grew as they neared the end of fourth grade.

But first, a little background. My hometown in 1967 had a total population of 150 or so, and is still holding at that count, even though our school closed twenty-five years ago. My class, most of us born in 1957, was the largest in the school's history, with a roster of twenty-one. We knew each other very well, and we were almost all related to several others in our class. It was a wonderful, tight-knit community, and we felt safe *until* fifth grade!

The elementary school was the two-story square, red brick building you so often see in small towns, with a large bell on a cement block near the front door. The rooms were small, but so were we, so we thought nothing of the fact that there might be thirty to thirty-five students packed in a room designed for fifteen or twenty, tops. Always, there were two grade levels in a classroom with one teacher. There were no helpers in those days, just one teacher.

We knew each other well, our joys, our families, even our birthdays, and also our fears.

Leaving fourth grade and Mrs. Truss, who was very calm and mild mannered, meant going into the classroom across the hall—to Mrs. Raatz's class.

Mrs. Raatz was at least eight feet tall and had striking short red hair, and she walked with a stride twice that of most people. Her voice was usually loud and echoed down the halls of our small school. When we heard it raised louder than the normal decibel level, we feared for the safety of our brothers, sisters, cousins, and friends in the fifth and sixth grades. Most of us would just put our heads down and pretend to study harder and pray she would move to another school before September.

Fifth grade—Mrs. Raatz—September 1967.

Safety in numbers, right? I'm sure none of us walked alone into the fifth- and sixth-grade classroom that first day, or even the first week. Mrs. Raatz, like most teachers, started off the first day by "laying down the law" and making her expectations known.

So it was true, everything we had heard … she really is mean!

Like our parents, she only expected the best from each of us, but she had a different way of saying it—always beginning with, "Now, boys and girls …" We quickly learned that if you messed up on your homework or a test, you would fear her wrath and probably endure it.

One of my brothers, during his time in Mrs. Raatz's classroom, messed up the only time in his life. He jumped the creek on our farm, in a hurry to get home for some of mom's homemade rolls, and fell in. He had been told not to take the shortcut and cross the creek, but to walk the driveway home with his little sister (me!).

When he fell in, so did his geography book, and overnight, it grew to three times its size. I don't even recall mom and dad punishing him, as they probably knew Mrs. Raatz would take care of it the next morning when she saw his book. I remember that he was scared to death, but I don't remember what happened, other than the fact that she kept that swollen book in her classroom closet for years, although I'm not sure why. It was certainly not usable. Perhaps it was to instill the fear in future students when they heard the story; maybe she used it as a prop when reinforcing her expectations.

Mrs. Raatz knew how to teach, and we learned the basics well: multiplication, long division, percentages, states and capitals, spelling, grammar, sentence structure. We always had homework, and many times, I fell asleep with a book or study papers on my pillow.

She expected us to work hard, but when it was time to play, we could play hard, and she often joined in with us, kicking the ball or swinging; she was such a kid at heart. In those days, teachers were free to hug their students, and she did that openly and often.

When we left her classroom for junior high, we were sorry to leave. It wasn't until years later that we would realize what a gift we had been given: a solid foundation of the basics needed in our education for a lifetime, I rely on that daily.

Now, when I look back, she's like Oz, the "man behind the curtain." It was all a game for her, and my, how it worked. Most of us left her classroom with the best two years of education we would ever receive in our lifetimes. The memories of her laughter easily drown out the shouts we used to hear in fourth grade—it was a fear factor, probably reinforced more by intimidation by older students, but only after they were safe and secure in the fifth and sixth grades.

In our little town, we were so fortunate to have many wonderful teachers, but few could match the colorful Dixie Raatz, who left a mark upon so many who walked across her classroom threshold.

Mrs. Raatz retired after forty years of teaching, almost all of them at Byron Elementary School. With her usual humility, she declined a retirement party, so a scrapbook was compiled and presented to her. It was filled with thank you letters and memories from former students over the years. She has often said that this scrapbook is a comfort to her on difficult days.

At the twenty-fifth anniversary of the school's closing, she was honored at a community gathering, and a skit was performed by former students in her honor. (Yes, my brother and a replica of the swollen geography book were a highlight of the skit.) I hope she continues to receive much comfort from the memories of being honored and from her scrapbook, as she was a blessing to so many.

As for that swollen geography book? I'm sure she really kept it for the many smiles each time she looked at it ... fear factor ... ha!

Evonne Williams is the Interim Executive Director of the Strategic Air & Space Museum. Prior to the museum position, she served as the President of Make-A-Wish Foundation of Nebraska for sixteen years. Evonne and her husband, Bill, have four grown sons and have called Omaha home since 1980.

A True Educational Egalitarian

by Peter Morrissey
about his High School Band Director, Doug Johnson

BAND—A CLASS THAT BEGAN as a chore, became one of my most enjoyable and rewarding pastimes. This is because Doug Johnson, or Mr. J, as we called him, is a man of magnificent skill and passion, and a man who doggedly pursues even the most disinterested musicians like me.

I am certainly one of those musicians who needs dogged pursuit, having endured, until high school, a rocky career in music. Despite nearly a decade of formal instruction and a great deal of time and energy devoted to two instruments, I was never able to develop the knack for performance that signifies a musician with a future. Meeting Mr. J on the first day of summer band, even before the start of the school year, is a memorable experience. It seems that with each passing year, as freshmen get smaller and more skittish, Mr. J becomes (metaphorically) larger and more ebullient.

My first meeting with Mr. J came with assurances that I was starting my musical career with a clean slate, and that the next four years would be of my own design. I was immediately taken by the man, so much so that I did not object when he called me "Pete," a name I would normally abhor (he would later dub me "Three-Pete" as there were three Peters in my class).

History buff that I am, I liken Mr. J's leadership of the band to the legendary big-city political machines of yesteryear. Though the bandroom was no Tammany Hall and Mr. J no Boss Tweed, he was able to command that same degree of loyalty from his bandsmen. Perhaps it was through use of a New York–style spoils system: bandsmen who had difficulty funding a band trip usually saw the fee waived, or who needed a higher quality instrument were loaned a school horn.

When 7:00 a.m. band became the norm every fall and spring, Mr. J frequently distributed cans of Pepsi ("Have a cold one, guys!"). Each year before a competition, Mr. J gave the same tried-and-true speech: "You know, there have been some great Prep bands, but this one, this one might just take the cake. If tonight you play like you've been playing, it's going to be one for the ages."

Even though I heard this speech every year, it did not lose meaning, but instead became more sincere. Despite this Richard Daley–esque combination of bribes and flattery, I am certain that our loyalty to Mr. J stemmed from something deeper.

At some point in his high school career, every bandsman's loyalty to this very time-consuming activity is tested; for many it ends in prematurely leaving the band. Well, my test came very early into my career, in October of my freshman year.

In the preceding few weeks I had really begun to find and enjoy my place in the trumpet section. On Halloween, Mr. J approached me outside his office and, while casually leaning against a door shuffling sheet music in his hands, asked me to give up the trumpet and learn a new instrument, the French horn. He explained that the overall balance of the band was trumpet heavy, and that I alone had displayed the flexibility and intellect needed to learn a new instrument in the middle of the year.

I, of course, interpreted it as, "Peter, you're bad. Go play a quieter instrument." As I wondered that week if this switch would be enough to drive me out of band, Mr. J made sure to seek me out in the halls and increase his already impressive dosage of confidence-inducing smiles.

At my first practice in the disorderly and much smaller French horn section, I remember somehow making kazoo noises emanate from my adopted instrument. Mr. J dubbed them "mellifluous," and I knew then that I could make it. The trust and confidence he placed in me, and in all of my classmates, was that deeper attraction that compelled our loyalty.

Three-hundred sixty-four days out of the year, Mr. J was calm, cool, content, and collected, whether that day holds rehearsals or concerts. Indeed, most days he is near jovial, with a memorable tendency for aphorism ("A band without tuning is like a one-legged man in an ass-kicking contest.").

But the one day that is the exception to this rule is the day of the District Music Contest in April of each year. Mr. J has good reason to be tense: his bands have received "superior" ratings every year for the past (as of this writing) twenty-one years, and every April he flirts with the disaster of blowing this record streak. On competition days Mr. J is extremely intense, the epitome of hardcore.

Though he never yells, Mr. J normally speaks loudly in order to be heard over the din of fifty-five instruments. But on DMC day, he speaks in barely more than a whisper. Instructions are instead written on the chalkboard and followed with hardly a thought. On the bus ride to the competition, Mr. J sits at the very front, staring straight ahead, uttering not a word. He avoids blinking in the hour prior to a performance. None of this should be a surprise though: hardcore means little to a marathoner like Mr. J.

While band was one of my extracurricular activities in high school, it was certainly not my only one. I ran cross country and did forensics for four years, and both of these activities routinely interfered with band. Mr. J was not angered that I frequently requested permission to shave off rehearsals to go run; instead, he asked when our next meet was so he could come watch. And every Friday when I told him I would be absent from Pep band to go to a speech tournament, he merely asked, "So who are you beating up on this week?" He was the first to arrive at my Eagle Scout Court of Honor and graduation party.

Perhaps Mr. J's understanding of *cura personalis* stems from the fact that he lives by that Latin mantra ("care of the whole person")—he is himself a marathoner, church music director, and devoted husband and father. Regardless of his motivations, it is significant to observe that in my class of bandsmen there were varsity football and basketball players, a state-champion wrestler, and a devoted bowler. He has the remarkable ability to see beyond his students' musical prowess and into the rest of their lives.

Perhaps the greatest musical character trait (some might say flaw) of Mr. J was his undying belief in the potential of *all* of his students, including that majority that does not want to pursue music as a career. Even though more than half of the students before him may never pick up an instrument again, Mr. J resists adopting a sort of musical triage (showering attention on those students "worth helping"). Instead, he fosters and demands the same level of excellence from all—a true education egalitarian.

Two of my classmates now major in music education, one of them at the prestigious Berklee School of Music in Boston. Both have expressed a quiet desire to be "the next Mr. J." A third attends St. Olaf Music School, majoring in performance. Another is now a trumpet in the Notre Dame Marching Band, and yet another plays clarinet in the United States Army Band at West Point.

As for me? Well, Mr. J affected me deeply as well: I am studying at Fordham University, majoring in history and secondary education.

Peter Morrissey is a student at Fordham University in New York, where he is studying political science. An avid debater, he has competed at the Oxford Union and World's Championships. He is deeply involved in the social challenges facing his Bronx neighborhood, working with disadvantaged New Yorkers to develop their job skills and continue their education. Morrissey is an intrepid traveler and hopes to work abroad after graduation before beginning graduate school.

A Teacher
Not to Be Forgotten

by Violet Popovich
about her Fifth-Grade Teacher, Dennis Murphy

DENNIS MURPHY WAS A nice-looking, tall, and friendly Irishman with a good sense of humor. His rosy complexion would become even more radiant when he needed to bring a noisy classroom to order.

His many talents were bestowed upon an energetic and diversified group including many high achievers with a desire to learn much from him. He was our teacher all day everyday and not only taught all the basic skills but also art, music, and physical education.

I loved the softball games because I and one other girl were considered good pitchers and also because Mr. Murphy gave equal support and attention to all of us. He taught with equal energy and interest no matter what the subject.

I admired his lovely handwriting and his perfect and interesting bulletin boards. When I finished my work early, he would ask me to help him with various tasks such as preparing the clay for art class or stripping a bulletin board for a new one. That made me happy.

We all liked our fifth-grade teacher very much and realized the feeling was mutual when he was granted his request by his principal to be our teacher the following year.

At a very young age, I would often say, "I want to be a teacher."

Mr. Murphy added inspiration and validation to that desire, which eventually became a reality.

Violet Popovich, a life-long educator, co-founded and subsequently became the sole owner/director of Beverly Hills Prep School for twenty-five years. The school provided an accredited college preparatory curriculum program for local and international students.

Irish Genius

by Dr. Richard Murphy,
about his Graduate School Adviser, Padraig O'Carra

I DID MY BACHELOR'S degree in chemistry and biochemistry in Cork, and then I went to Galway, which was another college of the National University of Ireland to do a PhD in biochemistry. This was a newly formed department of biochemistry with a very distinguished, albeit young chairman professor. He was my supervisor, but he was so busy in scientific and educational affairs nationally that he wasn't around often enough to give me the close supervision that I should have received in my area of scientific research.

When one year had gone by, I had not made a lot of progress, so my supervisor came to me with an additional, not alternative, project. So I was again left without supervision.

Soon thereafter, my supervisor asked a former colleague of his, Padraig O'Carra, who had just returned from a fellowship in Vienna, to keep an eye on me. And he did keep an eye on me as we would go and drink Guinness together. We soon became friends, going boating, and enjoying traditional Irish music together, in which we both had an interest.

We then formed a musical group that played together. I played the violin, and I discovered then that he wasn't just an incidental pianist; he was a true renaissance man—an accomplished artist and a scientific genius. He spoke German fluently and French manageably, and he could be comfortable in Italy or Spain. He further spoke as much Gaelic as English. It is his story and his influence I honor here.

We played a lot of music together with our musical group, and at the same time the science was going on. As I was getting through my school years in Galway, I needed to come up with a finding that addressed my hypothesis that there was a mechanism in plants similar to the mechanism in animals.

O'Carra was always looking over my shoulder and giving me advice. However, I didn't realize it at the time. I thought we were just chatting with each other as we were both interested in science. He gave me suggestions and criticisms, which is what research direction boils down to.

If you're going to train a young, independent philosopher-scientist, you must train him how to think logically, how to plan and study structurally and effectively, and then how to actually do it, in order to explain, in the end, what the results mean, what you observe, and what the observations mean.

It was only in retrospect that I realized that if I hadn't had the fortune of his coming back from Vienna, I would never have received a PhD.

O'Carra effectively, but not too gently, directed me. Opinions were stated forcefully and repeatedly at times, if necessary.

When I began writing my thesis, nothing that I ever wrote seemed to be correct. He wouldn't let me just sit down and write a paragraph. He found so many mistakes, not just with the construction of the sentences, but with the precision, accuracy, and logic of what I had seen, and my conclusions had to be related to what was to be known eventually.

Repetition of any kind was never tolerated. I remember one thing he asked me, and I do it now to my students. He asked, "How many times can you put something into a piece of literature?" The answer, of course, is once. Only once. When the information is in, it's in. You can't put it in again. And then he would point out to me, "Look, you have it three times in that paragraph." He had the uncanny ability to find and remember repetition even one hundred pages later.

In this collegial process, my thesis was completed and later we published it. Even ten years later, with O'Carra's continued help, we published two biochemical papers. O'Carra had been hugely productive in other areas of science and as a world leader. He broke new ground with many students and continued to demonstrate his strength as an investigator and as an accomplished scientist.

To me, he was a colleague, a fellow musician, and a consummate teacher.

Richard F. Murphy, PhD, born, raised and educated in Ireland, is Professor Emeritus of Biomedical Sciences at the Creighton University School of Medicine in Omaha, Neb.

Dr. Murphy joined the Creighton School of Medicine in 1988 as chair of the Department of Biomedical Sciences and was later named holder of the Peekie Nash Carpenter Endowed Chair in Medicine. He served as associate dean for research for the School of Medicine, 1991–1998. Dr. Murphy was responsible for combining Creighton's departments of anatomy, biochemistry, and physiology into a new Department of Biomedical Sciences, providing a flexible graduate research program and leading to greater interdisciplinary research and discovery by Creighton faculty, researchers, and student researchers.

Dr. Murphy has spent much of his career studying, writing, and lecturing on peptides, which in recent years have shown great promise for novel applications in medicine, biotechnology, and surgery. He has been particularly involved in the role of peptides in the prevention and treatment of diseases, including cancer.

The Gift of Learning

by Mary Beth Roderick
about her Second-Grade Teacher, Mother Boniface

WHEN I WALKED INTO Blessed Sacrament Grade School in Springfield, Illinois, in September 1958, I clung tightly to my mother's skirt. I wasn't ready to give her up for three hours each morning. However, Mom had a new home to decorate, my little brother to care for, and a very secure feeling that the nuns at Blessed Sacrament School would do right by me.

Mother Rose, the kindergarten teacher, gently untied me from my mother, pinned a name tag with a red bow on my dress, and led me over to a matching red chair by the window. Red bow, red chair. The first part of the first day seemed easy enough. The rules and routines were not so hard to remember and to follow. It was everything else that happened or didn't happen that flagged me as an early failed student.

I couldn't write the alphabet without leaving large erasure spots in the worksheet. Cutting out pictures and gluing them together seemed impossible. Standing up to recite a short poem brought me headaches and holes in my memory where words should have been. I got out of kindergarten, but only by the skin of my teeth.

First grade with Mother Monica was even more traumatic. I received my first book, part of the Cathedral series that several generations of Catholic children had used to learn to read. The Catholic version of Dick and Jane and Sally had wonderful pictures, with small words beneath them that I struggled to recognize and remember. Finally, out of sheer fright at taking my turn to read out loud, I begin to memorize words.

Like a first-year foreign language student, I didn't read to understand a concept or story. Instead, with my memory, I crawled over each word, as if it were a mountain to conquer. I made it into second grade, just barely.

I started the school year with a feeling of hope. I had heard from older kids in the neighborhood that Mother Boniface was nice. She was nice and looked younger than most of the nuns on staff. Her movements were quick and energetic. Her voice was clear, not cracked from old age. When she smiled, the smiles were smiles of genuine approval. She did frown and raise her voice, but only after real provocation. In short, she was a teacher to be trusted.

I began my familiar struggle in all things academic: reading, writing, math. Mother Boniface was patient, but firm. She believed that I could succeed. She praised me for small victories. She also insisted that I do work over, although with her help, I never fell hopelessly behind in my studies either.

In the days before the class of educators known as "Special Education" teachers, Mother Boniface had developed her own way of structuring her class to allow the advanced students to advance further, without leaving students like myself in a deep pit. I was beginning to see a faint light at the end of the tunnel, thanks to the wonderful woman in front of the blackboard.

For Christmas that year, I received a gift from my grandfather. Grandad gave me a book, one of the series of books based on a young French girl named Madeline. In the book, Madeline, who lived in a Catholic convent as a student, took a midnight trip to the hospital to have her appendix removed. I guessed at the story line because I had become an expert in reading through following the illustrations. But this story was different. I really wanted to read my new book, not just guess the story through pictures.

After the holidays, I took the book to Mother Boniface. I considered it a grown-up book and beyond the fairy tale books that I had on my toy shelf. Mother Boniface, with her great teacher's wisdom, sensed an opportunity. She told me that she knew about Madeline and wanted to read the story with me. If I would miss part of each morning's recess for a week, we could read it together. I agreed. We read together, out loud.

Several days into reading with Mother Boniface, I realized that I didn't have to point my finger at each word. And Mother Boniface had stopped reading with me. Finally, the words and the story ran together. I knew that Madeline survived, because I could read about her recovery!

Suddenly, Dick and Jane and Sally became my friends. I checked out books at the school library, not for the pictures, but for the story line. I eventually graduated to Nancy Drew, and then to Mark Twain, and on to Charles Dickens, Virginia Woolf, John Updike, never to be frightened of a book again.

Thank you, Mother Boniface, for all that you did, for your many students, including me. In an overcrowded classroom without air conditioning, computers, teaching assistants, and a variety of media resources, you gave the gift of learning through your daily acts of faith, hope, and charity to your students.

Mary Beth Roderick, a native of Springfield, Illinois, is a graduate of Western Illinois University. Her earliest educators were the Ursuline order of nuns and, later, the Springfield Dominicans. As a freelance writer, she has concentrated on local nineteenth-century historical subjects, in particular, African-American minority communities and their influence and impact on the larger society surrounding them.

You Can Do It!

by John Paul Engel
about the Woman Who Chose to Be His Mother

I WAS BORN WITH severe brain damage, addicted to drugs, and was deemed unadoptable by the state. The doctors said I would never walk. I would never have a normal life. I was supposed to spend the rest of my life in an institution.

Fortunately, I came to the Engel family—a family that took care of over 104 foster children over a twenty-year period.

When I went to school, I flunked kindergarten and was put in special education classes. Every day my mother would work with me at the kitchen table on my homework. Whenever I wanted to give up, she flashed me a smile and said, "You can do it!"

Did it, I did. I went on to earn academic scholarships to major universities. I became a competitive long-distance runner earning six varsity letters and winning 10k races in my age division.

I went on to graduate Phi Beta Kappa from the University of Iowa where I received the Collegiate Scholar Award—the university's highest academic honor. I worked on Alan Greenspan's research staff at the Federal Reserve Board. I studied under Nobel Prize–winning economists at the University of Chicago. I worked in twelve different countries with some of the smartest people in the world.

Yet the most important thing I ever learned from anyone I learned at that kitchen table. I learned from the woman who chose to be my mother.

She taught me to believe in myself and that has made all the difference. Today I share her message and advice from some of the most successful people in the world for free in speeches and in the book *Project Be The Change* (www.projectbethechange. com). Now anyone, anywhere in the world can get advice from some of the most successful people in the world.

Thanks, Mom, for believing in me when no one else did. Your belief made all the difference.

John Paul Engel is the founder of Knowledge Capital, a firm dedicated to helping companies achieve profitable growth. He began his career as an econometrician at the Bureau of Labor Statistics and then for the Federal Reserve System. He remains active in community service with interests in promoting foster parent programs, feeding the hungry, educating children, and improving health.

What Goes Around Comes Around

by Mark Andrew Gorup
about his High School P.E. Teacher
and Wrestling Coach, John DeGeorge

JOHN DEGEORGE WAS MY high school
P.E. teacher for my freshman and sophomore
years, and by my junior year, he was my weight-
training teacher. He was also well known as a
wrestling coach, as well as being an excellent
former wrestler himself. During my senior year,
I was his student assistant.

Our relationship turned into more of a
friendship rather than just a student-teacher
bond.

I remember that we would kid each other, and once in a while I would go overboard with lipping off, usually when egged on by my buddies.

One day, probably when I was a sophomore, I challenged him to a wrestling match, and he said, "Meet me in the wrestling room after school." I showed up with a few of my buddies and was pretty much humiliated by a middle-aged man whom I thought was out of shape. He put me down really fast and pinned me in about ten to fifteen seconds. Of course, everyone got a big kick out of it. I thought I could beat him, and he really proved me wrong.

I gained even more respect for him after that. The trash talk between us didn't end, but we both had an understanding that the talk was really a result of our friendship and respect for each other.

He treated everybody with respect. He taught us to treat people the way we want to be treated. He would often let us have fun as we worked in class, but never did it get out of hand. He didn't treat us like a number or a little kid. He was very easygoing and very easy to talk with, and you could tell he really cared about his students.

He retired from teaching a few years ago, after I graduated. He started a T-shirt business, and I started my own lawn business, so I went to his company to get T-shirts. We had many long and interesting conversations. After I sold my lawn business, I went into the business of helping people one-on-one in the health arena. I started doing personal training, and I still ordered my company shirts from him. He got me to join the local business association, and before we knew it, there was a role-reversal.

He wanted to get into better shape, so he hired me as his personal trainer. Instead of him making me run and work out, I make him run and work out. He works with me two times per week. He even has me working with his son to get him into better shape, so I've come to know his family better.

Our relationship is even better than it was back in school. It's pretty cool to still know someone from that far back who gave me advice when I was younger. He still gives me great tidbits of advice now. For example, my wife and I just had our first son, so he talks about family and raising kids. He still talks to me about starting a business too. It's really neat to see how the relationship continues to grow over the years.

When he introduces me to people, he says, "This is one of my former students. I used to make him exercise in P.E., now he's kickin' my butt and makin' me exercise!"

Mark Andrew Gorup is a franchise owner of Elite Performance Nutrition Stores, a nutrition business that excels in knowledge, products, and custom nutrition plans, as well as the President of Warrior Fitness, a fitness/nutrition organization that specializes in one-on-one fitness training and youth fitness camps. Gorup has been in the health and fitness industry for over four years and is an avid entrepreneur/ exercise enthusiast. He enjoys working with all individuals, young or old, and helping them live a healthier lifestyle.

My Pre-School Teacher

*by Cartney, age four,
about her Pre-School Teacher, Miss Margaret*

MISS MARGARET IS ONE of my favorites. She is fun and she is nice. She puts a "Dora" Band-Aid on us if we get hurt. She will hold us when we cry. Thank you, Miss Margaret.

Cartney's favorite colors are pink and purple, and she loves gymnastics and ballet. She also loves to play with her little brother, Ciaran.

My Own Pace

by Mary Dillon
about her Second-Grade Teacher, Mrs. Kosko,
and High School English Teacher, Mr. Gabriel

I'VE BEEN FORTUNATE TO have a lot of great teachers from kindergarten through graduate school. I have at least two that can qualify as favorite.

The first was my second-grade teacher, Mrs. Kosko. She was the first teacher who let me go at my own pace of learning, particularly with math. She pulled a couple of us students aside after the first few weeks of school and said, "Here's the book, work through the chapters on your own, and let me know when you have questions."

I remember thinking, "Really?" Not one to argue, I joined two others, at our own table, and started to learn second-grade math concepts. We went through the math book in a couple of months. She always made sure we understood the concepts, but she didn't let the rest of the class slow us down. She really encouraged us to learn the concepts and try to figure it out on our own first, and she was always there for questions or to check our work. Once done with the book, we moved on to the third-grade class.

It was one of the first times outside of my family that an adult showed trust and confidence in me. It was really a confidence booster to think that she knew I could do this on my own. Because she said, "You can do this," I rose to the occasion and moved forward.

To this day I try not to put limits on what people can do. I practice that at work, giving opportunities to junior team members to rise above and apply themselves to new projects or tasks. I have a higher level of expectations from others and definitely want to share that enthusiasm for learning and responsibility with my nieces and nephews. Hard to believe that such a lesson can be learned and carried forward at the age of seven.

Later, in high school, I had Mr. Gabriel as my English teacher for two years. Growing up where I did, it wasn't exactly a hot bed of culture or diversity. Mr. Gabriel was my first experience in getting to know someone with a disability: he was in a wheelchair from multiple sclerosis and, despite his difficulties, was this fantastic teacher who expected greatness from his students.

I remember being so impressed that he stayed so positive despite his physical challenges. Simple things sometimes seemed so difficult for him, such as operating an overhead projector or marking up papers. He often had to lift one arm with his other, just to place the transparency on the machine.

He taught us critical thinking skills and critical writing skills by reading and writing about the classics, making us earn with hard work our grades in the honors classes. Back in *my* day, there weren't spell-checkers or grammar checkers, other than human eyes.

Mr. Gabriel's red pen, which got pretty nasty at times, really taught me how to write and how to form arguments and thoughts while communicating with others. Not only did the critical analysis skills get me through my philosophy major in college, I still tend to be quite a stickler when looking for typos in my work or as I think about difficult challenges and how to solve them. He instilled those communication skills in me for life. He always pushed us to deliver, and that made us want to try our best.

Most of the time you don't get the opportunity to go back and recognize people who made an impression on you or helped set you up for success in life. Life happens. And time flies so fast. I know that Mr. Gabriel has passed away, and when I heard that, I was crushed. It's like a part of my own life has passed.

I think Mrs. Kosko would get a kick out of hearing how much I remember about her, and we could recount the story of the Christmas where I was entrusted with the hamster over Christmas vacation. The hamster did return safely, but there was a small period of time when his whereabouts were unknown.

Mary Dillon lives in Portland, Oregon, and works for Intel Corporation. She enjoys traveling the world, spending time with nieces and nephews, shopping for more photography gear than should be allowed by law, and finding the next great microbrew on tap no matter her location. She knows two things for sure: she's definitely a "dog person," and her favorite charity is the Make-A-Wish Foundation.

The Name Christopher

by Gail Houck
about her Fourth-Grade Principal,
Sister Mary Christopher

NOT ONLY WAS I one of eight children from my immediate family who attended my school, but it was the same school that my father and his eight siblings had attended.

Unlike my sisters, I was an average C student who was shy, chubby, and just wanted to help. Actually I thought for years that I wanted to be a nun when I grew up—the one that cooked at the convent and was nice to everybody. I outgrew that idea, but being the third child in my family,

I was still the helper, which was my safe niche. I volunteered early on to take things to the school office and always asked if I could do anything for them there.

I think I was in the fourth grade when we got a new principal, Sister Mary Christopher. She was very tall, at least to me at that time, and had a very stern and commanding voice, but a wonderful secret wink. Everyone was afraid of her except me. I thought she was great. You see, I had a dad with a stern, commanding voice and a wonderful wink, so I knew how to handle her.

Sister Mary Christopher recognized my need to be needed and with great care, kindness, and wisdom taught me that it was okay. I was the kid who often got accused of being a goody-goody or teacher's pet, and that hurt my feelings. My sisters often accused me of that and my insecurity with it grew.

Sister Mary Christopher taught me about people and the different gifts that God gives each of us. She made jobs and chores for me to do on weekends and evenings so that no one knew I would be helping. She was my special confidant, tutor, friend, and teacher. I always felt very safe and secure with her.

She was at our school until I was well into high school. After she left, I still wrote her letters until I lost contact with her.

What is amazing is that throughout my life the name Christopher has continually centered and grounded me. I left the town I grew up in and all my wonderful relatives to take a job in the South with the Sacred Heart Southern Missions. They are the fund-raising association that created the St. Christopher medal for safe driving, as St. Christopher was the patron saint of safety and security.

Once in Mississippi, I met my husband, Daniel Christopher, and we named our son Daniel Christopher. I truly wanted his first name to be Christopher, but our nephew Christopher had moved in with us, so we didn't.

We opened a personal care home for the elderly and one of the hardest decisions to make was to name the home. Yes, you guessed it; we named it Christopher's and our mission statement, of course, was "to provide safety and security with dignity for your peace of mind."

Now we have a resident pet Yorky dog whose name is Christopher, and he is one of the best additions we could have for our residents.

I want to thank my first mentor in life, Sister Mary Christopher, for continuing to light my path with special memories of her and the Christophers that have followed throughout my life. I would finally like to tell all who knew Sister Mary Christopher that she was really a teddy bear at heart.

Gail Houck is the proud mother of two wonderful children and the lucky "mimi" of two precious granddaughters. She currently resides in Holly Springs, Miss., where she is the owner of an assisted living facility of course named Christopher's. As a nurse for the last thirty-five years caring for others was wonderful but learning from the elderly has been a special blessing in her life.

I'd Grab Him
and Hug Him

*by Garrick Washington
about his Navy Chief Petty Officer,
Harley Davidson Whittle*

I WAS NAMED AFTER a President, and my
favorite teacher was named after a motorcycle.

Garrick. That's my first name. My last name,
Washington, is after the first President of the
United States. After the Civil War, there were
hundreds of thousands of former slaves with only
a first name. Lots of first names: Boo-Boo, Buster,
and Uncle Joe. But you couldn't keep a family
intact during the days of slavery. You could get
married one day, and your loved one would be

73

sold, and there was nothing you could do. It was really, really horrible.

So after the war, in order to give them a social security number, they started just naming them after Presidents: Washington, Jefferson, Jackson, and so on.

When I was in the Navy, my favorite teacher was Harley Davidson Whittle. Just like the motorcycle. His dad was an American Indian. His mother was European. He had very dark skin—not black, but olive-skinned. He was picked on a lot when he was growing up, so he developed a sensitivity toward those who are different. He was sympathetic toward blacks.

For me, it seemed like all you could be in the Navy was a cook or a steward. This was during WWII. Harley Davison Whittle was my leading petty officer. He was a country boy who grew up and hung out with the black kids. He was a person who was easy for me to relate to, and he didn't have the same hatred that others had.

My division commander, a commissioned officer, hated my guts. He asked, "How in the hell did you make E-5?" I said, "I passed the test." Boy that pissed him off. And that test is no easy thing to pass.

When Harley Davidson Whittle talked, he gave you graphic but simple examples. He was encouraging and complimentary. He said, "You are an E-5 petty officer now; you outrank over a third of all the enlisted men in the Navy." That was something I didn't know. He said I could leave on liberty every day at noon, while enlisted men had to wait until four.

Because I learned so much from HD and admired him, I started treating my men the way he treated me, and they liked me as much as I liked him. You can give directions and instructions without being stern and stiff and cold, even in the Navy. I'll always admire that man.

I've had no contact with him since I got out of the Navy in 1972. But isn't it interesting? Now, almost forty years later, he still is my favorite teacher. He made me feel hopeful. Up to that point, I began to feel that I was dumb, that I couldn't do anything. Because that's all I ever heard.

If Harley Davidson Whittle came up to me right now, I'd grab him and I'd hug him. And I'd tell him, "I love you." Because he made that big of a difference in my life—forty years ago.

Garrick Washington is retired from the Navy and has held many interesting jobs. He currently shines shoes in Chicago's O'Hare Airport, in Terminal B, "near the big dinosaur skeleton."

A Profound Difference in My Life

by Igor Seliazniou,
from the Republic of Belarus,
about his High School English Teacher

THE REPUBLIC OF BELARUS is a beautiful country. It has a population of about 10 million, and the land mass is about the size of the state of Kansas. It is surrounded by Poland, Russia, Ukraine, Latvia, and Lithuania.

The schools in Belarus have some similarities and some differences from those in the United States. While I think I received a good education there, schools in Belarus have a stricter schedule. They are harsher in telling you what you have to take, which leaves little room for what you want to take. Class size is usually around twenty to thirty students. Classes are set and more rigid in Belarus. Schools in the U.S. have more choices—I love the choices in U.S. education. There's much more democracy here in choosing what to study.

I graduated cum laude from Belarus State Economic University in 1997. I want to get a job in the financial industry in this country, so I'm currently finishing my MBA here.

My English teacher was my favorite. You see, English is a required subject in most of our schools in Belarus. It's such an important language for world business. My English teacher was so kind and knowledgeable. Teaching a language is much more intimate than teaching math or science or history. She really cared for her students and always went the extra mile to help us out.

She had a great sense of humor and she always seemed to be in a good mood. She had a high level of energy that was contagious. She didn't just teach a language, she also taught culture. In her classes, she included the history of English-speaking countries and told us interesting stories such as wedding traditions. She was a good storyteller.

She was also very smart. She not only spoke Russian and English, but also French and German. She was always open to critiques from her students and always strived to improve her teaching techniques. She prepared us extremely well for our final exams.

I try to visit her every time I go back to Belarus. I visited her when I went back this year. I can't imagine not staying in touch with her. She made such a profound difference in my life.

Dasvidania!

Igor Seliazniou, from the beautiful country of Belarus, drives a limo as he attends school in the United States. He speaks fluent Russian, English, and conversational Mandarin. After completing his MBA, he'd like to get a job in the area of international finance.

There Was Nothing I Couldn't Accomplish

by Billy McGuigan
about his High School Drama and Music Teachers,
Kent Hanon and Allen Barnard

IN MY PERSONAL AND professional life, I often wonder where and how I developed certain traits. My guess is that the bad traits that I have are innately unique to me, developed over many years of trying to undo the theory that I should know better. The good traits, however, were learned over many years of development. My professional traits and strengths can be tied to a singular year: 1992 and to two of my favorite teachers, Kent Hanon and Allen Barnard.

Hanon was a gruff and booming "larger than life" character. He had been a drama teacher at Bellevue East High School in Bellevue, Neb., for over twenty years. He also wasn't ashamed to tell you how great a run he had had as the overseer of the Bellevue drama program. He liked big shows. He did shows with casts of over a hundred that included everyone (freshmen to seniors, jocks to punks, preps to the poor kids) in school.

He demanded respect from all of his performers, and he got this by breaking them down and even berating them in front of crowds that would gather just to watch him run a rehearsal. He played no favorites and would relish in giving notes to and breaking down his star performer of 1992, me.

Barnard was a perfect gentleman. He was brought up in the old school manner of the 1940s and 1950s and had a calming demeanor that bespoke professionalism. He was the choir director at Bellevue East for thirty-six years and was wrapping up his career in 1992.

He had developed an incredible choral program at the school, and his choirs were a reflection of his remarkable attention to detail and meticulous attention to professionalism. He had worked side by side with Hanon as his musical director and was a perfect contrast to Hanon's need for the spotlight. Barnard didn't mind being the "sideman," as long as there was a place for everything and everything was in its place.

In 1992, I was a junior in high school and was starting to come into my own as an actor and performer. I was starting to shed some of that preteen gawkiness that had plagued me throughout my early teens. As such, I was cast in the spring musical as George M. Cohan in *George M*, and although this may have been expected because I was the lead the previous year, the task of playing a legitimate song-and-dance man was daunting.

First off, it was basically a one-man show. I was in all of the scenes and the eighty-eight-person cast that Hanon and Barnard had assembled revolved around and interacted solely with my character. Second, I had to sing 90 percent of all the songs in the show. Third, and most importantly, I had to be a proficient tap dancer. The only problem was that I had zero skills and experience as a dancer, let alone a tap dancer. What I didn't know then was that the three-month process of producing this show and the influence of these two extremely different men would profoundly affect me for years to come.

As a directing combo, Hanon and Barnard were themselves cast as a good cop/bad cop duo. Hanon would rip into me about my dancing not being up to snuff, and Barnard would pat me on the shoulder and tell me what a great job I was doing with the role. Barnard would work the songs with me during study periods and marvel at my work ethic, while Hanon would ignore the three to four hours of dance practice time I was putting in each day and tell me it wasn't quite enough. It was confusing to me as a seventeen-year-old, but it was effective. The sweat, tears, practice, frustration, dedication, and fortitude all paid off.

By opening night, I was ready to portray George M. Cohan in an extremely proficient manner: I could tap at a remedial level; my singing voice strengthened and delivered the songs with vibrato and gusto; and my ability as a performer grew enough to be able to lead the cast of eighty-eight to numerous curtain calls and standing ovations.

On the closing night of the show—Barnard's final show after thirty-six years at Bellevue East—the entire cast assembled in the choir room to receive our final pep talk prior to taking the stage. Barnard stood at the front of the room, flanked by his family and directing partner Hanon, as the speeches began. Hanon started first, delivering an eloquent homage to his creative partner of twenty years. The tears began to flow as everyone realized the finality of the evening's show.

After the cast and Hanon had composed themselves, Barnard began his farewell address. He delivered his speech with comedic flair, extreme humbleness, and he became quite emotional. It was the first and only time that Barnard had upstaged and outshined Hanon.

I learned so many things about myself that year from those two men while doing that show: I learned about dedication to my craft, and I learned that where there is adversity, there is also a shoulder for comfort. But the most important thing I learned was that if I applied myself totally, there is nothing that I couldn't accomplish. For that, I am eternally grateful to these two teachers.

Billy McGuigan is a nationally touring actor and musician. He has performed in over 400 performances of Buddy: The Buddy Holly Story *since originating the role in Omaha, Neb., in 2002, breaking box office and attendance records in six theaters across the country. He was chosen by the writers and producers of* Buddy *as their "Preferred Buddy Holly" in the United States. Billy has written, directed, and produced two nationally touring shows:* Rave On! The Buddy Holly Experience *and an interactive Beatles tribute show called* Yesterday and Today. *If you haven't heard of Billy, you will. He's a rising star on the national scene.*

Share Your Life with Them

by Frank Meeink
about his Sixth-Grade Teacher, Mr. Anotelli

EVERY FRIDAY, AT THE end of the day, my sixth-grade teacher in Philadelphia, Mr. Anotelli, would always teach us "common sense" things. For example, I was always big into sports. Of course I loved the Philadelphia Eagles. During football season, if the Eagles played the New Orleans Saints, he would teach us about New Orleans. If we played St. Louis, he would teach us about St. Louis.

He taught us little tricks about reading a map— things I still use to this day. He taught us things about the world and how to relate in it. Another trick he taught us was the nine times tables—that all the numbers equaled nine: for example, $9 \times 2 = 18$ (1+8=9), so it was easy to check our work. That made me want to learn more.

The classes were packed, and I'm sure we drove him nuts, but I really appreciated the way he taught.

I'm sure I wasn't one of his favorite students, because I was always getting kicked out of classes, including his, but the way he taught me has helped me help my son in school now.

I did see him years later and I had the chance to tell him he made a difference, even though I was bad in class. School was not fun for me, but he made it tolerable.

Today I would encourage teachers to show the kids that you care. Show an interest in their life. Ask the quiet ones questions to get them communicating more. Share your life with them and let them share their lives with you.

One of the biggest lessons I learned is this: The harder you work now, the less work you'll have to do when you get older.

Frank Meeink, featured in Autobiography of a Recovering Skinhead: The Frank Meeink Story as Told to Jody M. Roy, PhD, *in recent years has worked in a support position for professional hockey teams. He has been on the national lecture circuit for nearly a decade, speaking to various groups on the topic of racial diversity and acceptance.*

Commitment to Excellence

by Denny Lee
about his High School Latin Teacher,
Father Michael Hindelang

OF ALL THE TEACHERS I had in grade school, high school, college, and law school, which was a sum total of nineteen years of formal education, I probably would have had about a hundred and fifty teachers. And among all those teachers, one stood out.

His name was Father Michael Hindelang, SJ, a Jesuit priest, who taught me second-year Latin in high school. He was just the opposite of my first-year Latin teacher the year before. Father

Hindelang ran his classroom in a very particular manner. I thought, at first, that I did well in his class because I was afraid of him. He was one of those teachers who knew if you didn't come prepared for his class. He'd sense it.

You might be in the third row in the second seat back, but he would know that, of all the students in the class, you didn't do the homework and come prepared for class. He would pounce on you the entire class. It was like the Socratic method of law school with fifteen-year-old students.

But then upon further reflection, I realized it wasn't that I was afraid of him, but that I was afraid of disappointing him. Because of all the teachers I had over those years, he instilled in me, and in a lot of us, an attitude of excellence: to perform nothing less than the best you can do every day. Not only did I take that and apply it to his class, but that was really a foundation of my future academic success in undergrad school and law school.

It's also something I've tried to do every day professionally, and something I've tried to pass on to my three children. When he instilled in us that attitude of "do the best you can," that mediocrity was not acceptable, it was that attitude to which I aspire, even today.

He had one persona in class: that of being very direct, very stringent, and clear in his directions and expectations. He rarely laughed and never joked around during class. Being involved in activities after school, I would sometimes see a much different persona outside of class, as he walked his black Labrador dog, Jet. He couldn't be more friendly or jovial. He would always stop and engage me and other students in a conversation. He was interested in talking about you, and what was going on in your life, what were your challenges and goals. He knew how to give a boost of confidence.

His methods must have worked: out of the fifteen or twenty students in his class, most of us became doctors, lawyers, or priests, because Latin is a foundation language for those professions. One phrase, I'll never forget: *Omnia allia ex scrinis, prater steelum, ad shennagundum habnendum.* It would send shivers up your spine, because loosely translated it means, "Everything off of your desk, except your pencil; we're about to have a test."

About halfway through my first year of law school, I was taking the usual law school curriculum of constitutional law, property law, torts, etc. The biggest challenge was being told that only two out of three first-year law students make it to the second year. Halfway through the year I started to realize that I can handle this; I will be one of those who make it. And I realized this is the attitude that Father Hindelang taught his students when he took fifteen-year-old punk kids like me and helped us realize we could succeed if we worked hard, and we did.

Years later I received a call from him and he said, "Denny, this is Father Hindelang. You probably don't remember me, but ..."

I said, "Oh no, Father, I'm sorry to interrupt you, but I do remember you!"

Then he dropped the bomb. Out of all the students he had over the years, he asked me to introduce him at the induction ceremony. He was being inducted into my high school hall of fame. This was a few years after I completed law school. I was able to tell him then, publicly, that out of all the teachers I had in nineteen years of education, he stood head and shoulders above all the rest.

I spoke of his commitment to excellence. I told him and the audience that a good part of the reason for my success was directly related to the lessons he taught. I've tried to take his example and influence a new generation through my children and the people who work for and with me now. I try to give them the same lessons he gave to me. I like to pass on that we treat people in my office with dignity and respect, even when they perhaps deserve it the least. And you always do the best you can. It doesn't matter if you're six years old or fifty-six or eighty-six; if you apply those principles, you're going to have a good day.

Denny Lee is an Omaha, Neb., trial attorney. He believes that his personal and professional success is largely based upon his eleven years of Jesuit education beginning with his years at Creighton Prep.

The Glue That Binds

by Eric Crouch
about his Kindergarten Teacher, Miss Johnson

IT WAS KINDERGARTEN YEAR, and my very first teacher was Miss Johnson. There was this girl in my class (it always has to be a girl, I guess!), and we got caught eating glue. Rather than yell at us, Miss Johnson sat us down and calmly but convincingly explained, "We don't eat glue. It's bad for you and it can make you sick."

To this day I sometimes run into that girl and I say to her, "Remember when we ate that glue and got into trouble?" We both laugh when we think back on it.

After looking back over my educational career, I appreciated how understanding Miss Johnson always was. She never yelled or raised her voice. If her students would do anything wrong, she'd sit them down and explain why something was not acceptable. She was very good at what she did, and she had an excellent way of explaining herself to her young students.

There's no question that it takes a special person to teach kindergarten. I marveled at her teaching capabilities. When I look back, I think, *Wow! Kids at that age are so scatterbrained. To be able to coordinate activities with thirty of them at the same time is amazing.*

I very vividly remember the tremendous amount of patience she exhibited. I was able to tell her that recently because she invited me to her retirement party [after thirty-two years of teaching]. I was unable to attend the event, as I was playing football in Canada. But I wrote her a letter and told her how much I learned from her and that she was one of the ones who stood out as I thought of my teachers throughout the years.

Because she was so patient and set such a good example, I find myself to this day being influenced by her. I try to exhibit that same patience with my two young children. What a good role model she turned out to be.

She had a lot more influence on me than she probably even knew or imagined. And what she taught me will not just affect me, but my wife, my family, and my job. She also has the chance to affect my kid's kids, and their kids, and on and on and on. So I guess you never really know where influence stops. It can virtually go on forever.

Some things just stick with you (no pun intended). But what Miss Johnson ultimately taught me is the strong bond that holds a healthy life with good relationships together. For that I will be forever grateful.

Eric Crouch was born in Omaha, Neb., and attended Millard North High School. He is currently husband to Nicole and father to Lexi, age ten, and Carsen, age six. He graduated from the University of Nebraska at Lincoln in December 2001 and was drafted in the third round of the NFL draft. This Heisman-trophy winner played in four different professional football leagues from 2002 to 2008. Crouch currently resides in Elkhorn, Neb., and is owner of Crouch Recreation.

Teacher, Teacher, Burning Bright

by Rose M. Hogan
about her Junior High English Teacher, Sharon Moran

"CAN'T YOU JUST SEE the blazing eyes and feel the strength of the tiger? Can you picture how proud God would be of this magnificent creature?"

I did feel the clutch of William Blake's poetry and of so many other writers thanks to Sharon Moran, my English teacher when I was a junior in high school.

Ms. Moran's enthusiasm for the power of the written and spoken word ignited that same energy in her students, whether she was teaching literature or history or coaching the debate team. I was privileged to have her as a mentor in all three of those areas.

The main reason I became a teacher is that I enjoy working with young people. But the reason I chose a double major in literature and history— well, that has Ms. Moran's fingerprints all over it. I am now in my thirty-ninth year of teaching, and my priority has always been to convey that same joy of learning that Sharon Moran gave to me—the personal enrichment that comes from studying literature, history, art, and music; the confidence that derives from performing in speech, drama, and debate.

I love teaching, just as it always seemed to me Ms. Moran did. I hope I do justice to her inspiring influence.

Rose Hogan credits her late father, Jim Hogan, for her love of history and literature, and teacher Sharon Moran for showing her how beautifully those two fields combine. She retired in 2010 after forty years of teaching high school English, history, and humanities.

He Didn't Do Anything Other Than Be Himself

by Glen Howard about his Community College Algebra Teacher, Dr. Ropper

"YOUR BACKGROUND IS NO excuse not to perform in my class," Dr. Ropper once said to me.

He taught at a community college where I was returning to school as a non-traditional student. I needed a course that, quite frankly, I had reservations about taking. It was an algebra course that I took at night. Quite often I was exhausted from working my full-time job during the day.

Dr. Ropper was African-American, about six feet tall, bald head, probably around fifty-five or sixty years old, and he had a very "professorial" air about him. He spoke with perfect diction and pride and had an aura about being a teacher with a sense of passion and love for what he was doing. He cared about his students. He made sure you knew that the class was about you. As an African-American myself, it made me realize he was serious about teaching.

And he was very strict. He made no excuses that you would either pass or fail his course. For some reason, the way he communicated his care and concern for his students and their future really stood out. He recognized that his class was a step on the journey to receiving a college degree, and he took that very seriously.

Also, he didn't accept excuses for being poor, disadvantaged African-American students.

He didn't allow students to just come and take up a seat in his class. He took the attitude, "You're paying for this class, so I'm going to make sure you get something out of it." It was so evident that he cared about us and wanted us to take full advantage of our situation.

Some nights I would arrive in his class exhausted from working all day, and I would doze off. "Mr. Howard," he would call out with a deep, distinctive voice. And I would wake up. He would have me come to the board. I was never embarrassed, because he cared so greatly that we learned.

He would assist us at the board through difficult problems, so we could demonstrate that we understood and could work through the problems. It was his expectation that every student come to each class prepared. I was an okay math student all my life, but I got an A in his class because I earned it. He made sure I worked and earned the credit.

Outside of class, he was warm and friendly. He opened up his life, and therefore students would open up their lives, because he engaged in conversation with students after class. Even though it was nine at night, people wanted to stay because he was so interesting and interested in others. I learned not only math from him, but I learned how to teach adults, which I now do in corporate America.

Glen Howard lives in Henderson, Nev., with his wife, Debbie, and has a son named Nicholas who is a film student. Howard has a passion for life and a passion to motivate others to succeed in life. He currently works as a coach and corporate trainer. His core value is his passionate faith in God.

Class Clown

by Pete Lee
about his High School Science Teacher, Doug Pederson

"SOMEDAY, LEE, YOU'RE GOING to be on Comedy Central. I'm going to turn on that comedy channel and you're going to be right there!" My high school anatomy and physiology teacher in Wisconsin, Doug Pederson, said that to me so much, at first I'd think "no way," but then I'd start to believe, "Hey, maybe he's got something here."

I had struggled through my freshman year. Luckily, my sophomore year, I had Mr. Pederson as my science teacher. He just kind of impressed me the right way. The way he spoke was different than other teachers, and he was interactive. It helped that I was on the track team and he was one of the track coaches.

In class, I was always the class clown—giving a funny answer (and then the real answer). Instead of punishing me like other teachers did, Mr. Pederson said, "Oh my goodness, Pete, that was hysterical!" And he'd be happy about it and say, "Man, I needed a good laugh!"

He didn't talk *at* students, he talked *to* us. It was easy to connect with him. He didn't have a businessspeak or teacherspeak that a lot of people have. He used a normal vernacular. He was funny, too. He was definitely funny. That's probably why he appreciated humor. He'd sometimes start class with a five-minute humorous monologue, and then say, "All right ... on to anatomy!"

His positive attitude actually had a profound effect on me. I went from being a C or D student to an A and B student. I had more confidence because of him. I feel like I wouldn't have gone to college if it weren't for him. For a while I wanted to become a doctor or a psychologist, as I had a heavy science background because of Mr. Pederson.

But the comedy bug kept calling me back. I always said that if I ever made it onto Comedy Central, I'd write to him and thank him. And ten years later I made it. Then my local newspaper interviewed me, and I told the reporter that I tried to find Mr. Pederson, but he doesn't teach at my old school anymore. So I said to the reporter, "If you write about this, maybe this can serve as my thank you letter if Mr. Pederson reads this."

It turns out that Mr. Pederson worked with my brother back in my hometown and he said, "Tell your brother I read the article and that means a whole lot to me."

Pete Lee is a thirty-year-old comedian who lives in New York City. He is a headliner at clubs and colleges all over the country. He has appeared on NBC's Last Comic Standing *and his own* Comedy Central Presents Special. *He's definitely a rising star in the world of comedy.*

An Experiment in
Living and Learning

by Dr. Jim Schaffer
about his University English Literature Professor,
Robert E. Knoll

THE TREE STANDS TALL and straight in the Cather Garden near Love Library. A shagbark hickory. The tree is entirely unremarkable. No one would know that it was grown from a hickory nut found near Indian Cave.

No one would know the love and affection that tree represents either, unless, that is, the visitor were to kneel to read the inscription on a small silver plaque beside the tree, a plaque that reads

Arbores in lucis melius crescunt. In other words, trees grow better in groves.

The author of this inscrutable saying was Professor Robert E. Knoll, distinguished scholar of English literature and father of an experimental educational program at the University of Nebraska. The plaque was placed at the base of the tree by grateful alumni.

The Centennial Program, more often known as Centennial College, opened in September 1969 to celebrate the university's first hundred years. Centennial was also an attempt to meet the challenge of a new generation of students, a generation that demanded "relevance." Echoes of Vietnam and Berkeley were reverberating in Lincoln, Neb., that fall, and students complained that universities were making them numbers on IBM cards, anonymous to teachers and advisers.

Knoll and the other members of the Centennial Committee proposed an experimental college that would try to combine the students' academic and non-academic life into one experience. "We will have students living in the same building in which they attend class," Knoll said. "We hope their academic conversations will not stop when the bell rings."

The conversations didn't stop. When the new initiates to the Centennial experience arrived that September—125 freshmen and 52 upper-class students—they found a newly refurbished residence hall, which became the first co-ed housing unit on campus.

Workers had moved walls, put up partitions, and laid down carpeting. What they hadn't done was order furniture. An additional $2,000 had been set aside for the new students to choose their own furnishings. The money was never spent.

When the students arrived, they found a large Commons Room with thick carpeting, a large stereo, and no chairs or tables. They were delighted and insisted it be left as it was.

The "Grass Room" quickly became the focal point of Centennial activity. Townhall meetings were held there, where students debated what form of grading should be used. Visiting speakers—and there were many—addressed students there, and a new harpsichord, built by scholars themselves in one academic project, eventually settled in one corner.

"These kids don't live upstairs in their rooms," Knoll said. "They live in the living room."

"I thought the place smelled like a temple," recalls Knoll's office assistant Sally Gordon. "I thought it was incense, dumb me."

No matter what aromas emanated from the so-called hippie haven, students tackled their studies with gusto.

"I had always loved learning," recalls Kathy Cook, "but I always thought it was something I had to do in the privacy of my room."

Now students and professors alike posted study topics on large bulletin boards. Study groups formed, met for several weeks, and then disbanded, as students moved on to other topics or independent study.

Two weeks after the program began, one scholar left this message on the bulletin board: "I've been here two weeks and no one has talked about the weather."

Much of the college's disregard for grading and other traditional academic routines, Knoll said, came from disillusionment with the government's role in Vietnam.

"Centennial was the safety valve," he said, for the tensions caused by student unrest, but the college promoted an attitude of involvement and activism.

Twenty years later, when the Alumni Association sponsored a Centennial reunion, about ninety former scholars returned—now in their new personas as doctors, lawyers, teachers, engineers, and journalists.

"I had to worry about turning all of you free," Knoll told the alumni. "At what point did freedom become license and would your experimentation injure you? In fact, you might turn out worse than when you came in. But look at yourselves, look at each other. It's remarkable that you people turned into what you were all along."

The Centennial Program was disbanded in 1981, twelve years after its inception. In those years, 2,290 students participated in a brave experiment in residential living and learning.

"It had run its course," explained Knoll. "What we were doing was no longer necessary."

Perhaps the program was no longer necessary because by the early '80s the university had added independent study, interdisciplinary programs, and new dormitory arrangements. Today, the university provides fifteen different kinds of freshman learning communities.

But the lasting legacy of the program has to do with the sheer delight that Professor Knoll inspired in his students, a simple love of learning. As one young freshman in 1969 put it, "I have been asleep for eighteen years and have just awakened. It's wonderful!"

Dr. Jim Schaffer is a journalism professor at Nebraska Wesleyan University. He and his wife, Mary Lynn, a retired teacher, have two daughters and a son. Together with several colleagues he has written textbooks on speech, journalism, and most recently, creative writing.

A Kiss
Worth Waiting For

by Terry Redlin
about his Fourth-Grade Teacher

ONE OF MY FAVORITE teachers was my
fourth-grade elementary school teacher. She was
very young, in her twenties, and that year back
then was probably her first year of teaching. She
was also very pretty.

I learned the usual things: English, math,
geography, history, science, art, and recess. But I
also learned how pretty a teacher could be. Now
I wasn't obsessed with her, but I was very proud

to be taught by someone who I thought was the prettiest teacher in the whole school.

The year went by all too quickly—autumn, winter, and spring—and before I knew it, it was the end of the school year and time for summer.

On the last day of school, she asked the class to line up, as she wanted to say goodbye to each one of us and give us an end-of-the-year certificate. I purposely moved to the end of the line because I really did not want to say goodbye.

I watched my classmates in the front of the line. She gave out her certificate to each one individually and … wait … what else was she doing? She was kissing each student on the cheek! My heart raced. What a perfect way to end the year. It's a dream come true!

But wait again. As I observed further, I realized that she was kissing each *girl* on the cheek and shaking each *boy's* hand as she gave out her certificates. Oh, no! A handshake instead of a kiss? I came so close! My hopes were dashed.

Suddenly, a new thought seized my mind. Maybe by the time I reach the front of the line, she would start to tire. Maybe she would get mixed up and give me a kiss instead of a handshake. It's possible! I hoped and hoped and hoped and hoped.

But fate was not on my side that day. I reached the front of the line, and she did not forget, nor did she get mixed up. She gave me my certificate, stuck out her hand, and said, "Congratulations, Terry, you're now going on to the fifth grade." I shook her hand and slunk back to my desk.

Years later, after a successful career as an artist, I was honored when my son designed a museum to hold my artwork in my hometown. There was to be a dedication ceremony to commemorate the opening, and a guest list was made up. I had told my "almost kissed by my fourth-grade teacher story" before, so as a surprise, my family invited her to the opening ceremony.

She accepted the invitation. During the ceremony, there was a reception line to greet the guests. I kissed the ladies on the cheek and shook the hands of the men (my fourth-grade teacher had taught me well), and then she arrived.

She was still as pretty as ever. This time, she leaned forward and whispered in my ear, "Congratulations, Terry, your artwork is beautiful!" And then she kissed me on the cheek.

It's a great feeling to be complimented by a former teacher. My heart raced. A lifetime had passed since I longed for that kiss. My wish was fulfilled. My fourth-grade teacher still holds a very special place in my heart. It was a kiss well worth waiting for.

Terry Redlin is an internationally acclaimed artist from South Dakota. His work is a vision that celebrates the wonderful variety of American life. It is the remembered story of real people, everyday things, and a beautiful landscape that is uniquely ours.

A Little Bit of Passion Goes a Long Way

by J. Medicine Hat about his High School History Teacher, First Boss, and Dad

MY FAVORITE TEACHER IS a three-way tie—each person had a significant influence on my life.

I was not into school at all. You look at my report card, and it would read D, C-, C-, American History A+. History was the only thing I excelled at. I used to get D minuses in Phys Ed! There's a lot more to life than climbing that darn rope!

But my high school American history teacher, Ray Devlin, made history terribly fun for me, and

I've had a lifelong passion for it since. I just can't get enough of history. I can't read enough about it. I can't remember very well, except for history stuff. I have an unbelievable knack for dates. I can retain historical facts, but I can't tell you what I had for lunch yesterday.

When I travel to perform, I get to my hotel room and turn on the History Channel, and it doesn't get turned off until I leave town. Even when shows are repeated, I watch a second or third time, and I get even more out of it then. So much history stays in my head. How? I don't know.

I expressed an interest to Mr. Devlin about Native American stuff. I could tell at the time he was restricted on what he could teach—like it had to be straight from the book. But he encouraged me to go to the library. He encouraged me to read *Bury My Heart at Wounded Knee.* That's what got me very interested in my heritage.

I was kind of a trouble-maker. So I didn't get a lot of respect from other teachers, as it should have been, because I was a rotten bastard. But Mr. Devlin just caught me.

After I graduated, I ran into him a couple of times. He'd ask, "How's that comedy thing coming?" I made a point to tell him what a positive influence he had on me, and it really seemed to make his day.

I told him my goal was to do six minutes of Thanksgiving material on the night before Thanksgiving on the *Tonight Show with Jay Leno.* That would be perfect. I've had friends ask me, "Are you celebrating Thanksgiving tomorrow?" I'd tell them, "Only if you're paying. The last time my people celebrated, it cost us a continent."

See? A joke like that is funny, but it makes you think. I truly believe that Native Americans are the forgotten people. We have no voice. Some people seem to think all the Indians that were in this country are dead. Mr. Devlin encouraged me to research my heritage, which in turn encouraged me to keep this topic alive.

Then there was Lou Murray, owner and operator of Murray's Chick Store. He was such a big influence on me that, when I bought my first house, I got a glass door to put on my office, and

I stenciled "Murray's Chick Store" onto the glass window. That's how much he meant to me.

He was the owner of the store and my boss. He was incredibly good with people. He sold young chickens to raise, and people would come from many miles around because they would only buy from him. There were sometimes 100,000 chicks in boxes, and you had to feed them and water them real fast. He was nice to a fault.

His favorite saying was, "Remember to remember and forget to forget." And he had another saying, "Give me turkey when I'm hungry, champagne when I'm dry, a good woman when I need her, and Heaven when I die." I've never forgotten that.

We worked hard, but we also played hard. I learned more just by watching him: how to talk to people, how to make people feel relaxed, how to sell to people. He always wore a hat and long coat. He was in his sixties, and one day I saw him pick up a 50-pound sack of feed with one hand, step up to the counter, and set it down effortlessly!

My third influence was my dad, Earl Monk. He had seventeen brothers and sisters and grew up in a family where they had nothing. My grandpa was a garbage man. So my dad had to work. And he worked hard. He used to tell us boys, "You gotta learn how to work, boys, because you'll be working at least until you're sixty-five. Find something you like, something you're good at."

He worked harder than any other human being I ever met. And that's what killed him. He died at forty-two of a heart attack when I was twenty-one.

Finally, since this is a teacher-focused book, teachers need to make it interesting! You gotta put some bait on the hook! A little bit of passion goes a long way.

J. Medicine Hat is a nationally recognized Native-American comedian from the Midwest. Medicine Hat is his grandmother's maiden name. He appears regularly at Funny Bone Comedy Clubs and other venues around the country.

Canadian Idol

by Kate Whitecotton
about her College Theater Teacher, Nancy Sager

MY IDOL WAS MY college stage management teacher, Nancy Sager. I had her for two years as I worked on a theater degree in Canada. She was the best!

She was not only my teacher, but she was a mentor and later became a very good friend. Not only did she teach me in class, but she guided me through several practicums. She was the production stage manager for all of the main stage shows at our school. I got to work alongside her and observe what she did. And she did her job better than anyone I knew.

She had worked in theater for years, and she was living proof that one can make a living doing what she did. She worked in a lot of theaters, on cruise ships, and in other venues. Not a lot of people understand what I do, but she has lived that life. She completely gets it. She's very smart on the business side of stage management, and she passes business knowledge and books on to me. I always admired her experience. If I have a problem, I would just give her a call, and she would help me.

Stage management is a cut-and-dried business; there's not a lot of room for interpretation. She really knew her stuff and was very serious in class in making sure we learned what we needed to learn. So in class she was one thing, but outside of class she was perhaps the funniest person I ever knew.

During shows, she was always in control. When she needed to, she would pull me aside and say, "You need to pull it together because you're not doing your job right now." I really respected her for that, because she didn't just always take it easy on me. She made sure that all of her students learned what we needed to learn.

When any one of us made a bad decision, she would let us know and tell us we had to fix it ourselves. But she was always there for support. She was motherly, in a teacher sort of way. She taught us a lot of people skills, too. She taught us how to deal with different personalities. When you work with people in the arts, on and off stage, you have a variety of types. What she taught me then really helps me get along with all different types of people now.

We're such good friends now, she knows how very thankful of her I am. That's why she's my idol, because we've moved past the teacher-student relationship into an actual friendship that's equal. There's a genuine respect between us now. And for that, I'll forever be thankful.

Born and raised in Red Deer, Alberta, Canada, Kate Whitecotton is the production coordinator for a very successful production company called Rave On Productions. Kate tours all across North America with the production company. She enjoys running, playing tennis, and hanging out with her friends.

He Made Me Feel Special

by John Lauer
about his Tenth-Grade Shop Teacher,
Paul Grundstrom

PAUL GRUNDSTROM WAS MY air conditioning, heating, and refrigeration teacher in the tenth grade.

From the first day in his class, I knew he and I would get along well. He always took time to make sure we all understood what he was teaching and made the class interesting and fun.

As time went on, Mr. Grundstrom and I formed a friendship. I could talk to him about everything, and he would always give me great advice. There was never a time that he was too busy to help me. I can remember times when he would help with other classes that I was struggling with. He would also help with personal struggles.

The best memory I have of Mr. Grundstrom was when he asked me to help him with remodeling a home he had purchased. He made me feel as if I were one of his sons. I spent weekend after weekend working at his home making money and learning.

It was then that I first learned to paint. I have been painting ever since. Mr. Grundstrom made me feel very special in a difficult time in my life. I had kept in touch with him for several years after, and then he had moved away. I will always remember how much Mr. Grundstrom meant to me.

John Lauer is from Clearwater, Fla., and has lived in that area for thirty-two years. He has been married to Grace for nineteen years. They have two children: John, Jr., twenty years old, and Elizabeth, ten years old. He is a property manager full-time and handyman and painter part-time.

That Magical Blend

by Bary Habrock
about his High School Social Science Teacher,
Dan Bormann

WHILE I HAD MANY excellent teachers, the one that stands out most in my mind is Dan Bormann—my mentor, my coach, and my high school social science teacher.

From the beginning, I admired him as a leader who was positive, very real, and empowering. I always respected the way he listened and the way he led through example. He had the ability to influence through his moral, intellectual, and social interactions. He talked to everyone with great respect, especially his students. This was probably the first indication that made me want to follow his example.

In the classroom, he had a command of content, classroom organization, and time, which led to high-level student engagement. When leaders use time well, that sends subtle messages that they are serious, passionate, and purposeful about their craft. For him, as a coach, this led to high expectations and an excellent ability to motivate his players. His conversations always seemed to be rooted in mutual respect. He was so purposeful in what he did in the classroom and what he did as a coach.

He helped shape me not only as a person, but how I am as an educator. I believe that the success of the school is explained by the human spirit of educators who possess the magical blend of belief in cause and dedication to mission. He was a great model with a magical blend of relationships and dedication to mission, which he leveraged to get the most out of kids.

Because of his influence, when I approach relationships and conversations with kids, I am thoughtful and purposeful about it. I try to emulate his ability to connect with kids through mutual respect. Conversations matter and are critical to all relationships, while serving as our sole mechanism for meaningful change, growth, and connection.

For me personally, Dan Bormann showed his willingness to go out of his way to engage in meaningful conversations. Those conversations motivated and stuck with me. Not only the content of the conversations, but just his willingness to take the time to engage in those conversations.

In the end, he motivated me to write my future story. He pushed me to set higher goals for myself because he saw potential that I could not yet envision as an adolescent. That's what I appreciate most.

He taught me so much in the classroom because of his focus on the content and outside of the classroom because of his relationship, attitude, purpose, and mission. He just had that magical blend.

Bary Habrock is the assistant superintendent of Elkhorn Public Schools. Bary's wife, Ronda, is a high school math teacher and was also positively impacted as a former student of Dan Bormann. Together they believe in the power of high expectations and connection with young people.

It's About
Lifting People Up

by James Malinchak
about his High School English Teacher, Mrs. Monaghan,
and Assistant Basketball Coach, Randy Marino

I GREW UP IN a small steel-mill town near Pittsburgh, where I played basketball. I was lucky enough to get some recruiting letters from a few colleges, yet a lot of people around town told me, "Oh, you're not quick enough," or "Nobody from our town has ever done that."

Even though I was pretty much a positive kid, if you hear the negatives long enough, you start to believe it. Then one day before English class, my teacher, Mrs. Monaghan, could tell I was down, and she asked, "Is everything okay?"

I told her I was starting to get letters from colleges for basketball, and I was beginning to feel that I couldn't do it and I was getting down on myself. I told her how everybody seems to be telling me I'm not quick enough, I'm not big enough, I don't come from a big town, and I told her, "You know, they're probably right."

Mrs. Monaghan, a nice lady, a very sweet person, then got up and came around her desk and got right in my face and said, "It's ridiculous for you to believe those people and think you can't do this." She then told me a Walt Disney quote I'd never heard before: "'If you can dream it, you can do it.' So stop listening to those people and just go do it!"

Here we are, twenty years later, and I still remember her and those words like it was yesterday. What an impact that made! Those words helped me get a college basketball scholarship. And I later wrote about her in a book for teenagers called *Teenagers Tips for Success*.

Randy Marino, a substitute teacher and assistant basketball coach, always believed in me too, even when I didn't believe in myself. He's actually now the principal at the school I graduated from.

Since basketball was my passion and kind of my way out of the small town, he would constantly encourage me. I would always be talking about all the big-time players in Pittsburgh high schools, and he would say, "Yah, but you're leaving somebody out, because *you* are one of the best players in the state."

I'd say, "Come on, Coach, it's just me. I'm from a small town. These are kids from the big city."

But he would again encourage me. He was a great leader of young people because most young people want someone to believe in to follow, and somebody who believes in them.

My mom and dad, never very financially well off, taught me the importance of character, integrity, and a good work ethic. My mom would wake me up in high school at 5:30 so I could go to the gym and work out to become a better basketball player. She did that every day! She made sure I had food and that I was warm on those cold Pennsylvania days, and she drove me to school. Never once did she complain. She could have said, "Hey, catch the bus at 7:30! 5:30 is too early!" But she didn't. She did that for me.

Now my dad, as a teacher, would never tell me what to do. Which I think is an incredible leadership quality. He used the Socratic method. He always knew the answer, but he would say, "Well, what do you think," or "How can you overcome that challenge," or "How are you going to get through that?"

He let me figure things out on my own. He was the most even-tempered man I have ever known. He would never get overly excited or mad. At my basketball games, he would just sit there and watch. He was a Division I football referee and basketball referee, so it wasn't like he didn't know what was going on. He just wanted me to grow by figuring it out on my own.

I use that technique when teaching others to this day. As I mentor and coach other people, sometimes I let them figure it out on their own. It means so much to empower others, like my dad empowered me. What a teacher he was!

It's so important to be a teacher of life, because you never know how one line spoken or one simple act of kindness shown can influence someone for the rest of their lives. That can make all the difference in the world. Words and actions can spring someone up to a higher level or slice them down like a hot knife cutting through butter.

As W. Clement Stone said, "Little hinges swing big doors." As teachers, we are leaders. And leadership is not about power, it's about empowerment. It's about lifting people up instead of stifling them and pulling them down. Teaching is leadership.

James Malinchak grew up in a small Pennsylvania steel-mill town and has gone on to become one of the "Most Requested, Highest Paid Motivational Speakers in America!" He also teaches others how to become a highly paid motivational speaker. Learn more about Malinchak at www.Malinchak.com and www.BigMoneySpeaker.com.

She Pushed Us to Think for Ourselves

by Nick Ingraham
about His College Biology and Research Professor,
Michelle Mynlieff

COLLEGE WAS FILLED WITH fantastic memories, grueling hardships, invigorating successes, disappointing failures, endearing friends, and unforgettable mentors. Each aspect would prove their importance in keeping my sanity throughout the four years, but it was not until now (after graduation) that I can reflect and fully appreciate the magnitude of how lucky I was to become part of a particular community within my university.

Late in my sophomore year, I sat down with the dean of the biological sciences department and found help in ending a two-year search for the right major: physiological sciences. This became my first step into the community of the biological sciences department of Marquette University, which, unknown to me, would become a second family that was full of generosity, opportunity, and resources that seem to have no end.

During my junior year I was continually urged by members of the department to apply for their summer research program. Scientific research had never seriously crossed my mind at that point, but my current classes in the department had sparked an interest. I decided to apply and serendipitously fell into the best situation I could ever have asked for.

Dr. Michelle Mynlieff, coincidentally my freshman year biology teacher, was brave enough to take me into her lab for Marquette's summer research program. The program was the best thing I did in college. I was able to get to know many of faculty and staff in the department. It was a whole new experience.

Through research, symposiums, and poster sessions, I realized the respect every faculty member and graduate student gave to the undergraduates. I did not feel like a student anymore; I was an amateur scientist who had much to learn and benefit from their knowledge; while at the same time, I brought a little to the table myself. It was apparent the enthusiasm they had as scientists, which was matched by their passion to teach us along the way.

Dr. Mynlieff and her lab—two graduate students and an undergraduate—provided an atmosphere that could not be matched. It was expected that I ask too many questions, learn from my mistakes, and enjoy every minute at the same time. Day in and day out I never once felt as if I were at school or work.

I would leave my family at home to begin the day with my family in the lab. Dr. Mynlieff cared for us as her children while at the same time expecting nothing less than our absolute best.

She pushed us to think for ourselves while gently guiding through all the disappointments that come with scientific research.

At the end of the summer my family came into financial issues that could have hindered my return to Marquette University. Without my even knowing it, she called the financial aid office seeking options that allowed me to finish my education at Marquette. Later that spring, when she heard that I had been wait-listed at a medical school, she immediately asked for the address of the admissions office to send in a follow-up recommendation letter. And she graciously made room in her grant for me to work for her that summer as a research assistant.

These are just a few of the amazing feats that Dr. Mynlieff did on my behalf. I cannot express what she has done for me literally or how she has served as a model for what a mentor/teacher/supervisor/friend should be.

I will never forget the kindness she has bestowed upon me and everyone else who is blessed to become part of her life. I will never meet a more amazing women who was able to push me academically just as far as she has pushed me to becoming the man I am today.

Nick Ingraham recently graduated from Marquette University majoring in physiological sciences. He attends Creighton Medical School and plans to become a primary care physician.

Finding a Favorite Teacher Twenty Years Late

by Elayne Savage about her High School English Teacher, Marcia Blacker

I WAS TWELVE YEARS old when my mother and grandmother died in a plane crash.

I was pretty much a mess for a few years. Alone and adrift and afraid. Each day reflected the blur of the day before. Through the haze of those years, a few people tried to reach out. I pushed them away. One person stands out in her effort to reach me—my high school English teacher, Marcia Blacker.

I was disruptive in her class. Whispering, blurting out without raising my hand. Lots of acting out behaviors. I guess I was trying to get some attention.

One day she asked me to stay after class. She wanted to talk to me. *Groan.* I plunked my belligerent self down in the chair next to her desk, expecting to be chewed out. But there was no lecture. Instead she asked, "Is anything wrong at home?"

I was speechless.

In fact, there was a lot wrong at home. But I just couldn't bring myself to tell her about how miserable I was or about how I was trying to hold things together for my dad and my nine-year-old brother. How my dad sold his business and took a job traveling the state. How he hired a housekeeper to take care of us. How she used to bounce me from one wall to another of the basement.

But somehow Mrs. Blacker noticed something might be wrong. And she was the only adult who asked that question: "Is anything wrong at home?"

She tried to be supportive. She was the first person to encourage my writing and submitted one of my class stories to a community writing contest. I remember I wrote about an orphan who wanted to be adopted.

According to the rules of the contest, she had to assign a pseudonym for judging purposes. To this day, whenever I have to quickly come up with another name, I use that pen name: Anna Franklin.

Over the years, I have remembered her kindnesses. Yet, it wasn't until many years later that I fully understood the importance of this special teacher in my life. I was in my forties and working on a PhD in Family Therapy. My schizophrenia class met for a day-long experiential class.

The class spent the day on the grounds of a retreat site. We paired off. We were to take turns playing two roles: the "crazy one" who could be anything we wanted and the "keeper" who made sure the crazy one stayed safe. The instructor, a local psychiatrist, was always nearby.

He passed out blank name tags. We were to choose a name and an age to write down. I found myself writing the age "fifteen." Then I spontaneously wrote the name "Marcia." For the next couple of hours, I was fifteen years old, experiencing old emotions and scary thoughts.

At the end of the day I realized I had chosen that age for a reason. When I was fifteen, I was having trouble holding things together. I was probably on the brink of breaking down. I also realized the name I chose was the name of my high school teacher, Marcia Blacker. She was my teacher when I was fifteen. Isn't it amazing how the mind works!

I knew I needed to find her, but I had little to go on.

I remembered her husband was in medical school. I remembered his name because he was once a counselor at my camp. My instructor guided me in finding her by locating him. Physicians are very easy to find anywhere in the country.

I found Marcia Blacker, in Lexington, Kentucky. I recorded and sent her a tape of my memories of those high school days. I told her how grateful I was for her concern. It was hard to record. I kept crying and flipping off the tape when I couldn't speak clearly.

What prompted her to ask that question? I needed to know what she remembered about the day she decided to ask me about my life at home.

Her response came. I was disappointed. She remembered me as a bright student. She did not remember that after-class conversation or what might have led up to it.

A short time later her son, David Blacker, published a book for aspiring teachers. He included my story. As it turns out, he collected memories about her influence on students. The transcript of the tape I sent her is in his book, *Dying to Teach: The Educator's Search for Immortality.*

Back in those high school days, Mrs. Blacker was a grown up and I was a kid. In reality there were only a few years' difference in our ages. At the time I was in her in junior English class at Central High School, she was freshly out of teacher's college.

Ever since I found her, we've stayed in touch. Can you imagine what a thrill it was when I was giving a book talk in Louisville, Kentucky, and she drove in from Lexington to hear me speak! The best part, though, was when I introduced her as "the first person who believed in my writing ability. I'd like you to meet my high school English teacher, Marcia Blacker."

Dr. Elayne Savage is a communication and workplace coach, psychotherapist, professional speaker, and author of Don't Take It Personally! The Art of Dealing with Rejection *and* Breathing Room: Creating Space to Be a Couple. *She is the go-to person on how not to take rejection and disappointment so personally.*

Shaping the Future

by Tom Osborne
about his College Literature and College History Teachers

I HAVE TWO FAVORITE teachers from my education at Hastings College.

One was Daryl McFerren. He was a history professor. I majored in history. So I had Daryl for probably six or seven courses, which varied from World History to American History to Russian History. I was always impressed with the depth and scope of his knowledge and his ability to be prepared. He was an excellent communicator.

History could sometimes be pretty boring, but Daryl made it come alive.

The other was Elizabeth Bowen. She taught literature and Shakespeare. I only had a couple of courses from her. She also was an excellent communicator and really an impressive teacher in terms of her knowledge of her subject matter. Elizabeth really made Shakespeare come alive through added insight and anecdotes to her teaching that made it very interesting.

Both of these people were there to teach. Their focus was not on research or writing books, although I believe each of them did some writing. They were very effective teachers for under-graduates and were always very approachable to students, which students really appreciated.

Obviously, they came across as people who cared, who really wanted their students to do well.

I would hope that I would come across to my students, like they did, as someone who is interested in each of my students, that I care about them beyond just having them as students sitting in my class and interested in their doing well, not just in class, but in life. I hope I project to them that I will spend extra time with them in the regular office hours I maintain.

I think students really do appreciate approachability. I have fairly large classes, and sometimes it's difficult to maintain the level of personal contact one would like, but a number of students would come in. I believe I was able to maintain a good level of communication with them.

One thing I've always enjoyed about coaching is the interaction with young people. My stint in Congress kind of took that away, and now teaching has allowed me to renew that type of activity.

Communication with team players is important. Everyone is different, and everyone can certainly make a contribution, and you want to encourage them along that line.

I think teaching is perhaps as important a profession as there is, because you're shaping young people and their future. In turn, you are also shaping the future of your country. A good teacher can make a tremendous difference in the long-term well-being of the country and, ultimately, the world.

Dr. Tom Osborne was the head football coach of the Nebraska Cornhuskers from 1973 to 1997 and won three national championships. He then was elected to the U.S. House of Representatives from the state of Nebraska, where he served three terms. He currently is the Athletic Director at the University of Nebraska.

A Powerful Influence in my Life

by Lydia Burgos
about her High School Principal, Sister Dolores

MANY TEACHERS HAVE HAD a positive, powerful influence in my life. I was born in Panama City, Panama. At age seven, my family moved to the small town of Puerto Armuelles, on the border of Costa Rica, where my dad worked for the Chiriqui Land Company, an American company in the business of cultivating the Chiquita bananas and exporting them to the United States. Dad was the paymaster general. There the company hired English-speaking teachers to teach in the little three-room rural school in Puerto Armuelles.

One of my English teachers, who came from Montana, would often talk to us about having to go to school knee-deep in snow. I was fascinated with snow. I would ask her, "What is snow like?" and she would reply, "Imagine living inside your freezer!"

To a kid who did not like the heat and humidity of the tropical country's climate, "living inside the freezer" sounded like heaven!

The opportunity arose for me to come to the United States when the company offered its employees the perk of giving their children, who qualified, a free ride on their banana boats to ports in the United States and the promise that if the student did well in an American or Canadian accredited school during the first two years of high school, the company would pay for the next two.

Before long I was on one of those banana boats to New Orleans, and then I took a train ride north. And that is how I came to Omaha, Neb., to go to school at Notre Dame Academy, a high school run by the Notre Dame Sisters.

Everything was new for me and for the Sisters. I was the first foreign student in their midst. I was amazed at how little English I really knew, and they were super kind and helpful, always teaching me, always caring for me like the child or grandchild they never had. Because I was the oldest girl in a family of six girls and two boys, it had been ages since I was treated like a child. Needless to say, I ate up all the attention they gave me.

It was toward the end of my junior year when Cuba had fallen to Fidel Castro and the political speculations were that the next country Russia was interested in was Panama because of the Canal. I got a letter from Mom telling me why they had not written as faithfully as they had done in the past. There had been an uprising in the plantations. One of the paymaster generals on the Costa Rica side had been beheaded in one of the plantations.

An underground paper ran an article that was titled, "Know Your Enemies." Our dad's name topped the list. He was outspoken against the way they were carrying out their protests against the United Fruit Company and had succeeded in convincing some to turn away.

I was very upset with that letter and took refuge in the Notre Dame chapel where I could not contain my tears. Some of the older Sisters who were in the chapel alerted Sister Dolores, who was principal of the school and a very good "take charge" kind of person—a genuine problem solver.

Sister came to me and asked me to come into her office. After listening to me translate my mother's letter, she looked at me very seriously, her piercing blue eyes almost looking through me to my heart and soul. I knew she meant what she said and I believed her. She said, "The same thing that happened in Cuba is going to happen in Panama. Do you think that, if we can help, your family will leave Panama and come to live in the United States?"

I said I did not know but that I would ask. When my dad got my letter, he and Mom discussed it, and they decided that if the Sisters were willing to help us, my family would indeed move to the United States. Because of their connections, by the beginning of my senior year my mother, my sisters, and my youngest brother, a third grader back then, were in Omaha.

Sister helped us find a house near Notre Dame Academy so we could walk to school. A year later, she got the wheels in motion again and got Dad to come to Omaha as things were not improving in Panama. The rest is history.

In later years, Sister Dolores always kept contact with the family. She always wrote at Christmas time, and whenever we visited Notre Dame she showed another side of her. She was no longer the Principal persona of my youth, but a kind, loving, funny, genuine friend, who was very interested in me, in my family, and in our accomplishments.

Sister Dolores de Notre Dame was born in Omaha of Czech heritage. I learned later that she was instrumental in helping others escape Communism. Perhaps, this is why she so keenly understood the threat my family could face. All my family's lives changed dramatically because of her.

I became a Spanish/French teacher and taught school for thirty years before retiring to establish myself as a translator/interpreter. One of my sisters became a nurse; another holds a master's degree in public administration; one is a well-respected, knowledgeable technician in the heart catheterization lab at Alegent Health in Omaha; yet another, a retired supervisor from Mutual of Omaha; and the baby of the family works with computers and has also held supervisory positions.

Sister Dolores's reaching out to help has touched our lives down to the second generation of the Burgos family. She holds a very special place in our hearts.

P.S.: I still love snow and cold weather much more than hot weather. As I grow older, however, I've learned to respect that power of Mother Nature and rather enjoy her display from the picture window inside my home.

Lydia E. Burgos, born in Panama City, Panama, came to Omaha, Neb., on a scholarship to attend high school at Notre Dame Academy. She enjoyed a successful career teaching Spanish to students from third graders through middle school, high school, and college. This multi-award-winning teacher is now retired but continues to work on her business, Burgos Translations, offering the community her services as translator/interpreter, voice-over talent, and director.

Una influencia poderosa en mi vida

Por: Lydia Burgos,
Directora de una Escuela Secundaria

Since Lydia Burgos is a professional translator, she translated her story here for our Spanish-speaking friends.

MUCHOS DE MIS MAESTROS y profesores han tenido una influencia positiva y poderosa en mi vida. Nací en la ciudad de Panamá. A los siete años, mi familia se mudó al pequeño pueblo de Puerto Armuelles en la frontera con Costa Rica, donde mi papá trabajaba para la compañía Chiriquí Land Company, una compañía estadounidense que se dedicaba al cultivo del guineo, o banana, para exportarlo a los Estados Unidos y al Canadá. Mi papá ocupaba el cargo de pagador general. La compañía empleaba maestras norteamericanas para que enseñaran en la pequeña escuelita rural de tres aulas en Puerto Armuelles. Una de mis maestras era de Montana, y a menudo nos contaba que ella tenía que caminar a su escuela hundida en la nieve hasta las rodillas. Yo estaba fascinada con la nieve. Le preguntaba, ¿cómo es la nieve? y ella me contestaba diciéndome, ¡Imagínate vivir en la congeladora de la refrigeradora de tu casa! Para una chica a quien no le gustaba la calor y la humedad del clima tropical del país, vivir dentro de una congeladora me parecía ser ¡la gloria!

Se presentó la oportunidad para que yo viajara a los Estados Unidos cuando la compañía les ofreció a sus empleados la gratificación de darles a sus hijos, que calificaran, el viaje gratis en sus barcos bananeros a cualquier escuela secundaria, acreditada, en los Estados Unidos o el Canadá y la promesa de que si el / la estudiante lograba aprobar bien los primeros dos años la compañía pagaría por los últimos dos años de la secundaria.

Un poco tiempo después me tocó a mí viajar en uno de esos barcos a Nueva Orleáns, y luego tomar el tren hacia el norte. Y, así fue que llegué Omaha, Nebraska, para asistir al colegio de Notre Dame Academy, un internado bajo el cargo de The School Sisters de Notre Dame.

Todo era nuevo para mí y para las Hermanas. Era la primera estudiante que venía de un país extranjero. Al comienzo me asombraba darme cuenta del poco inglés que hablaba. Yo sólo sabía que las monjitas eran muy amables y muy dadas a ayudarme, siempre enseñándome, siempre cuidándome, como la hija o la nieta que nunca tuvieron. Siendo yo la hija mayor de una familia de seis hembras y dos varones, hacia ya tiempo que a mí me trataban más como adulta que niña y, por supuesto, que me encantaba toda la atención que recibía de las monjas.

Fue a fines de mi quinto año de secundaria, comenzando la década de los años sesenta, cuando Cuba cayó en manos de Fidel Castro y las especulaciones políticas eran que el próximo país de interés para Rusia era Panamá, por el Canal, que recibí una carta de mi mamá donde me decía el por qué no me había escrito en tanto tiempo como lo había hecho en el pasado. Había habido un levantamiento en las plantaciones. A uno de los pagadores generales del lado de Costa Rica le habían cortado la cabeza en una de las plantaciones. Había salido un periódico clandestino en el que habían escrito un artículo titulado, *Conozca a sus enemigos.* El nombre de mi papá encabezaba la lista. Él había hablado en contra a los que protestaban contra la United Fruit Company y había logrado convencer a muchos que desistieran de protestar de la manera que lo estaban haciendo. En cualquier caso, me molestó mucho la carta y busqué refugio en la capilla de Notre Dame en donde no pude contener las lágrimas. Algunas de las Hermanas muy mayores que se encontraban en la Capilla alertaron a la Hermana Dolores, quien era la Directora del colegio, una persona muy buena en hacerse cargo de las situaciones, en tomar decisiones y solucionar problemas. La Hermana me buscó y me pidió que fuera con ella a su oficina. Después de escuchar mi traducción de la carta de mi mamá, me miró muy seriamente, sus penetrantes ojos azules me miraron directo a mis ojos con una mirada que parecía penetrar a través de mí a mi corazón y a mi alma. Sabía que no estaba jugando y le creí. Me dijo: Lo mismo que le ha pasado a Cuba le va a pasar a Panamá. ¿Piensas que si nosotras le ayudamos tu familia se viene a vivir a los Estados Unidos? Yo le contesté que no lo sabía pero que le iba a contestar la carta a mi mamá preguntándole esa pregunta. Cuando mis padres recibieron la carta, ellos hablaron sobre la oferta, y decidieron que si, en verdad, las Hermanas estaban dispuestas a ayudarnos a salir del país, mi familia sí aceptaba venir a los Estados Unidos. Por sus contactos, al comienzo de mi sexto año, mi mamá, mis hermanas y mi hermano menor, de tercer grado, en aquel entonces, llegaron a Omaha, Nebraska. La Hermana Dolores nos ayudó a comprar una casa cerca de la academia para que pudiéramos ir a pie a la escuela. Al año, la Hermana Dolores puso de nuevo en marcha el proceso para traer a papá a Omaha ya que las cosas no parecían mejorar en Panamá. El resto es historia.

En años posteriores, la Hermana Dolores siempre mantuvo contacto con la familia. Ella siempre escribía en Navidad y siempre que visitábamos a las Hermanas de Notre Dame llegué a conocer su otra cara. Ya no era el personaje, serio y fuerte, de mi juventud que dirigía el colegio de Notre Dame, sino una persona amable, cariñosa, divertida, una auténtica amiga, que estaba muy interesada en mí, en mi familia y en nuestros logros.

Hermana Dolores de Notre Dame nació en Omaha, Nebraska de patrimonio Checo. Más tarde me enteré de que ella fue instrumental en ayudar a otros a escapar del comunismo. Quizás, por eso es que sentía tan profundamente la amenaza a la que mi familia podría enfrentar. Las vidas de todos en mi familia cambió radicalmente gracias a ella. Fui a la universidad y obtuve mi maestría en Educación Secundaria. Me convertí en profesora de español y de francés y ejercí la profesión por 30 años antes de retirarme para establecerme como traductora e intérprete. Una hermana se hizo enfermera, otra tiene una maestría en Administración Pública, otra, es muy respetada, en su trabajo como técnica con conocimientos en el laboratorio de cauterización cardíaca en los hospitales de Alegent Health, otra más, se jubiló después de muchos años de trabajar como supervisora en la Compañía de Seguros, Mutual of Omaha, y ahora ocupa una posición de encargada en una agencia para ayudar a los pobres, muchos de ellos hispanos, por lo que su habilidad de hablar español es una ventaja. El hermano más joven se unió a la Infantería de Marina y sus dos hijos también son marines. La bebé de la familia tenía 5 años cuando la familia se mudó a Omaha, ella se ha desenvuelto trabajando con computadoras y también ha ocupado puestos de supervisión.

Así es que, al tenderle la mano a mi familia para ayudarnos, la Hermana Dolores tocó nuestras vidas hasta la segunda generación de la familia de Burgos. Ella ocupa un lugar muy especial en nuestros corazones.

P.D. A mí todavía me encanta la nieve y el clima frío mucho más que el caliente. Sin embargo, al envejecer, he aprendido a respetar el poder de la madre naturaleza y más bien disfrutar su exposición desde el ventanal de mi casa.

A Little Encouragement Goes a Long Way

by Forrest Gregory
about his High School AP Biology Teacher,
Dennis McDermott

DENNIS MCDERMOTT WAS MY high school AP biology teacher my senior year. He was funny. He knew how to relate to students, and he had a good sense of direction in telling you what to do so you could get good grades.

He was very energetic. He would get up at five in the morning or earlier to run. In class he'd write on the chalkboard so fast that we students would take notes as fast as we could. We would just try to keep up with him and process massive amounts of information. Then he'd stop and crack a joke to relieve the tension, and everyone would laugh. It took the pressure off for a minute, and then he'd get right back to the material.

He was really good at telling you the material from a book perspective and analytical angle, but he also was good at breaking down the material with diagrams and pictures to make it more understandable than the book did. That catered to left brainers and right brainers at the same time.

He was very dynamic and open about all kinds of scientific theory. He encouraged us to have our own opinion about things and didn't try to cram his opinions down our throats. He encouraged us to think for ourselves, which I think everyone really appreciated. He'd give guidelines, but he let us discuss our theories and opinions about things too. He was very open and accepting of all people and things. For instance, we would sometimes go outside for class when we were learning about plants and photosynthesis. It was like a lab situation.

This was the first class in the morning, so one morning we watched the sun rise in the east. We were supposed to observe and write down what we thought was going on. He would say, "Look at how the leaves are facing and look at how the plants are bending. They are actually facing toward the light because they are trying to absorb as much sunlight as possible." He added that if we were to come outside at five or six p.m., then the sun would be in the west and the plants would be bending the other way.

Another example is when we dissected cats in class. It was a massive amount of information to retain from the book, but he had a way to break down the information to make a difficult task seem easier. I have to say I remember more information from his class than I did from any other class in high school. Again, it was the way he related to us that made all the difference. He was energetic and excited about his subject, and he made it fun to be in his class. Yeah, I loved biology, and that was part of why I liked the class, but he increased my attraction to the subject and made me want to go into that field all the more.

In high school, I was known as "the Discovery Channel Science Guy." My senior superlative that I received from my classmates at the end of the year was "most likely to save a whale." I wanted to be a marine biologist. Mr. McDermott knew that, and he helped me out by being himself, being who he is, and sharing his passion, especially with those of us who were developing a similar passion.

At the end of my senior year, I asked Mr. McDermott to sign my high school yearbook, and he not only signed it, but he wrote, *Forrest, Your interest in the environment is more intense than any student I've ever had. I hope you stick with it! I learned a lot from you this year. Thanks and take care, Mr. McDermott.*

Forrest Gregory graduated from Doane College in 2008 with a bachelor's degree in fitness management. He is currently in college at the University of Nebraska at Omaha, completing prerequisites to become a physician's assistant.

My School in Poland

by Magdalena Gorzyczka
about her teachers in Poland

I'M FROM A SMALL town in Poland called Wronki. It is famous for having the biggest prison in the whole country. It's a very historical prison, which housed prisoners from WWII. My brother actually works there now. I came to the United States about two and one-half years ago to study English and to go to school. Right now my major is business management.

I met my fiancé here. He's from Poland, too. My grandma told me that's the reason God sent me here, "To meet a Polish man to marry." We'll go back to Poland to get married.

In this country, I noticed the relationship between teachers and students is different. Teachers are closer to their students here. In Poland, the relationship seems stricter. For example, in this country you can call your teacher by name. In Poland, you must address them as *Professor* or *Sir* or *Ma'am*. It's much more formal.

My Polish teacher, Barbara, was actually very strict, but she was a very good teacher. Not only did she teach me Polish, but she was my coach for school speech competitions. She was an excellent role model. She told me she was proud of me, and that made me want to do better. She taught me how to be more self-confident and brave. She was very special to me. She spent a lot of time with us on how to make presentations better, and she had us attend her other classes to practice our speeches. I wanted her to be proud of me because I really liked her.

Another teacher, Monika, was very young when she taught me. Because she was young, it seemed as if we could talk to her about anything. Most of us took the bus to school, but when we missed our bus, she would offer to give us a ride home. She was very open and involved. This was the first time I experienced this.

She was more like teachers in the United States. They really care about the whole student, not just the subject. She was like a friend for us. She taught accounting. She also likes to travel. I keep in touch with her online. She still gives good advice, like "Don't stay engaged too long!"

I ask her how her current students are and that I hope they love her as much as we loved her. I can tell that makes her feel good. She tells me that it is harder to teach now, because many students don't appreciate what they have. Teaching is getting harder, she said.

Magdalena Gorzyczka is an international student from Poland. She recently graduated from Metropolitan Community College in business management and is continuing her education at Bellevue University. She is currently the owner of a small business called Pine Commercial Cleaning.

She Let Me Develop My Thoughts

by Tom Becka
about his Seventh- and Eighth-Grade Teacher,
Sister Marlene

WITHOUT EVEN THINKING, I can tell you right now, my favorite teacher was Sister Marlene. I went to a Catholic grade school in Columbus, Ohio, and Sister Marlene taught the seventh and eighth grades.

This was during the Vietnam War, and she was a very socially conscious nun. During history class she would sometimes have us read the newspaper and talk about current events. For example, she got us discussing the plight of the Mexican farm workers and Cesar Chavez in California. Even though now, in hindsight, some of my political views have changed from the ones she held back then, she got me thinking and interested and engaged.

She also had a great sense of humor. She was fun. She was funny. She was also very energetic. She would never bore you. I could challenge her on things, and she would let me. She would make me support my thoughts. Some conversations even carried over after class. A lot of teachers would have told a student to just listen, but she let me develop my thoughts.

She opened a youth center so kids would have somewhere to go after school. I remember going there and helping her paint it. Now this was the late 1960s, so we painted it fluorescent colors and used black lights and played rock-and-roll music. She would welcome that! Other teachers would have said, "Oh you can't do that!" But not Sister Marlene. She let us make decisions and carry through with them.

At the time I thought she was about a hundred and twelve years old, but now, in hindsight, I think she was only about twenty-one or twenty-two. She would not criticize us for being young, like a lot of the other teachers would. This would sometimes get her into trouble with some of the parishioners.

She also taught me the next year during eighth grade, and some of the parents tried to get her kicked out of the school because of her teachings. She was anti-war, and some of the parents didn't agree with that. I didn't realize until much later how proud I am of my dad, because he was one of the parents who stood up and said, "No, she is here to challenge all kinds of thinking and to get her students to think for themselves. I support her being here."

Most of us probably carry a little bit of all of the teachers we had with us throughout our lives, but I know I carry a little more of Sister Marlene with me than any of the other teachers I had. So, Sister Marlene, if you're reading this, give me a call. I'd love to carry on our conversations.

If I saw her right now, I'd say, "What the hell are you doing here, Sister? We're in a bar for God's sakes!" Actually, I'd say, "Thanks! Let me get you something. Sit down! Let's talk some more. What do you think of what's going on in the world today?" I'd love to have the chance to carry on a conversation with her, adult to adult.

Tom Becka is a nationally recognized radio talk show host. He can be heard throughout the Midwest on KFAB and on www.KFAB.com. Prior to his career on the radio he toured the country as a standup comedian where he opened for Jerry Seinfeld, Sam Kinison, and the band Chicago, among others. He is also an author and motivational speaker. His book is There's No Business Without the Show.

He Had Faith in Me Even When I Didn't Believe in Myself

by Jennifer Di Ruocco
about her Graduate Professor and Adviser,
Dr. Peter Smith

WHEN I FIRST MET my professor and adviser Dr. Peter Smith, I was beginning my graduate program in education. I walked into his office with a sheet of paper where I mapped out the thirty-nine hours I'd need to receive my master's degree.

He knew me through my résumé and graduate school entrance process and through the Alice Buffett Outstanding Teacher Award I'd received. There I sat in his office, being a mom, a full-time teacher, and now a student; I wanted to receive my degree as quickly as I could. I wanted my higher education to be quality, but I wanted it to be on a fast track, because I didn't want to take any more time away from my husband, kids, or students than I had to.

When I showed him my schedule that was mapped out to take all thirty-nine hours in just eighteen months, his first reaction was, "Wow! Generally people take two to two and one-half years for this program."

"No," said I, "Eighteen months."

He said, "Okay, eighteen months then."

That was the beginning. He never discouraged me, he always encouraged me. He stuck by my side and understood that I was determined. I explained why I had everything mapped out for eighteen months. He took the time to listen to me then, as he would throughout the next eighteen months, no matter how busy he was.

He understood that we had lives outside of school. I appreciated that he saw me for the kind of person I was. He took notice of the personality types of his students and related to us appropriately. He also treated us as professionals, which we were. He knew we had experience, but he also knew we wanted to better ourselves. He always used kind words, had a gentle smile, and a sense of humor.

In a class like Interpersonal Relationships, he would break it down and use real-world examples. He would let his students think and take the time to share real-life experiences. He always respected the opinions of others.

He shared stories of his own experiences as an educator, as he came up "through the ranks" of being a classroom teacher, then supervisor and an administrator in public schools. He had walked in our shoes, so he could relate to real-world experiences.

I would rarely miss class, but the couple of times that I was absent, he understood we had a life outside of school. One time I had to go to the hospital, and when I returned, he was genuinely interested in how I felt. He was concerned about my well-being. I, on the other hand, was worried about class, but he wanted to make sure that I was all right.

When I would be so stressed about taking twelve hours in one summer and completing a comprehensive examination, he put me at ease. I was really nervous and wanted to know how I'd done on the pass/fail exam. I saw him a few days later and asked if he had the results, and he said, "No, I'm sorry, I don't have the results yet." I was going to have to wait another week before I received the results letter in the mail. I said thank you and headed for my car in the parking lot.

I typically am in a hurry, but for some reason that day I moved more slowly than usual. I slowly walked to my car, slowly opened the door, slowly got in and opened the window, and slowly started to drive away. As I looked out my car window, I saw Dr. Smith running across the parking lot motioning to me.

"Jen, Jen!" he yelled as he flagged me down. I stopped and asked him if everything was all right, and he said, "I just checked my voice mail, and you passed!" He ran all the way down the stairs and across the parking lot to tell me the news, because he knew how important it was to me. He said, "Now you go home and enjoy the weekend!"

He always had faith in me even when I didn't believe in myself, whether it was a test or project or whatever. He knew I always set such high expectations (and so did he), but he always demonstrated his belief in me. He was very good in connecting theories with the real world, and with connecting one class to another. He made sure students were prepared when they left his program.

The last class I had with him was a curriculum course. After the course was finished, he came up to me and said proudly, "Well, you did it." I know why he said that. He remembered my going into his office eighteen months prior and announcing that I wanted to complete the program in eighteen months. Once I put my mind to something, I usually go for it. But I got help along the way. I was lucky to have a supportive husband, supportive kids, a supportive principal at my job, and even supportive first graders.

But with all this wonderful support, when times got rough, it was Dr. Smith who first said, "You can do it!" He reminded his students that we knew more than we sometimes thought we did. It's like the pieces of a puzzle. He'd show us that they were there, and then he'd guide us in putting them together.

He showed such passion for education. He looked for ways to improve education and challenged us to always look for ways to improve education, too. He held high standards. In short, he is the professor that I try to be as a teacher.

Jennifer Di Ruocco is a wife, mother of three, and a first-grade teacher. She received her master of science degree in educational administration and supervision (in eighteen months). This Buffett Teacher Award–winner has a passion for the future of our kids in this world. She believes kids are precious, and we need to raise/teach them with care, as we only have one shot at it.

Connections

by William Kloefkorn
about his College Literature Professor, Green D. Wyrick

HE WAS A TALL handsome man who stood erect at the front of the classroom, an open book in his right hand, a smile somewhere between wry and self-satisfied on his lips. His hair was a light red, straight and stringy, and from time to time he'd pause in his reading and move several wayward strands from his eyes with incredibly long fingers. He reminded me a lot of Errol Flynn, that swashbuckling Hollywood icon who never failed to hold my boyhood attention.

My professor spoke and read slowly, and with an intensity—a passion—that surprised me.

Though I was a sophomore, I was nonetheless a greenhorn, an unwashed *honyock* who really didn't know his derriere from his elbow, though thanks to my having enrolled in five credit hours of French as a freshman, I did know the meaning of *derriere.*

The professor surprised me because, for one thing, he was male, and, for another, he talked about literature and read poems aloud without making any excuses or apologies. For me, this was unfamiliar territory.

In high school my English teachers were female—three of them over a four-year span. I liked them, especially the youngest, who handled upstarts like me with untold patience and finesse. My experiences with these teachers led me to the naïve conclusion that all English instructors were female.

As I have already admitted, I was probably the greenest freshman ever to have enrolled at Kansas State Teachers College in Emporia. So when a tall, handsome man stood straight as a rake handle reading, say, Edwin Arlington Robinson's "Mr. Flood's Party," I was first embarrassed, then amazed, then finally and forever impressed.

And not only was he male, he was delivering the poem as if by god the poem mattered, as if what was happening to the old man might somehow be relevant to my own life. Well, of course it decidedly was not relevant to my own life. I was a young man. Eben Flood was an old man, old enough to have outlived his contemporaries. From time to time he'd climb the hill near the town where he had spent much if not all of his life, and with a bottle of hooch in tow, he'd have a little party, all by himself. Politely, he'd offer himself a drink, and just as politely he would accept it.

The professor read the dialogue, much of it from memory, as if he had written the poem himself. I remember these lines especially: "The bird is on the wing, the poet says, / And you and I have said it here before. / Drink to the bird."

A footnote in our anthology informed me that Mr. Flood was quoting from Omar Khayyam's

Rubaiyat. Our professor, having finished reading the poem, suggested that we find a copy of Khayyam's book and read it, whereupon we entered into a discussion of "Mr. Flood's Party."

Our professor led us down paths I had not much appreciated in the poem—the relentlessness of time, the brevity of human existence, the meaning and worth of dignity. The old man in the poem has outlived his contemporaries, and no doubt his own life is nearing its end. But he perseveres; he has yet enough physical toughness to climb the hill, and enough intellectual acumen to acknowledge his mortality by alluding to an eleventh-into-twelfth-century Persian poet who once upon a time also acknowledged, and wrote about, his own mortality.

So I was impressed with my male professor's interest in the poem, but also with his relating it to what others had written about the same themes. "Human dignity," he said. "It's what Ernest Hemingway said that all of us strive for—to live and to die with dignity."

Now I had not read very much while attempting to grow up in south-central Kansas. My chief literary influences were these: (1) the Sears & Roebuck catalogue; (2) the King James Bible; (3) comic books. Ask me about the shirt section in Sears & Roebuck. This shirt is good. This one is better. This one is best. Ask me about Sampson and Delilah, David and Goliath, Saul of Taursus, King Herod, Ruth and Boaz, Philemon. Ask me about Billy Batson, the Torch and Toro, Batman and Robin, Superman, Wonder Woman, Captain America. But don't ask me about—well, about anyone of literary merit beyond the covers of Sears & Roebuck, the King James translation of the Bible, or comic books.

With the exception of Ernest Hemingway. When my professor mentioned his name, and spoke of a connection he had with a deceased Persian poet, I was virtually stunned. Yes, I had heard of Ernest Hemingway. He had come to me by way of a copy of *Life* magazine in which the short novel first appeared. The magazine lay on an arm of a green bench in Urie's barber shop, along with a copy of J.G. Taylor Spink's *Sporting News.*

I had a lot of time to kill—early Saturday afternoon, a truckload of farmers ahead of me, waiting to have their own ears lowered—so, having devoured the *Sporting News* (the Dodgers were losing again), I picked up the copy of *Life.* A picture of a full-faced bearded man was on the cover. He was smiling and holding a red rose. I was struck by the picture because the face, in spite of the smile, did not seem to me to reflect the type of man who'd be holding a red rose—or a pink one, either, or yellow or any other color. But there it was, the face of a rugged individual whose full-fleshed hand was holding a red rose.

I thumbed through the magazine. When I reached the page where Hemingway's story began, I stopped. I read the brief introduction, then the story's first sentence: *He was an old man, and he had gone eighty-four days without catching a fish.* I continued to read. It was an easy story, its language simple and straightforward, and the subject of fishing was one I could relate to. Almost an hour later, when Urie called my name, I was already well into the book. Reluctantly, I laid it on the green bench and took my place in Urie's huge familiar chair.

I finished the book that same afternoon in the Rexall drugstore, where I sat in a booth with a chocolate malt and a copy of *Life* I had borrowed from the rack along the north wall near the pinball machine. I was sorry that Santiago's big fish was eaten by the sharks, but I was happy that he had put up such a courageous fight. He had said that you can kill a man but not destroy him, which somewhat confused me—until that day in class when my professor talked about the subject of dignity. I was all ears. Yes, I had heard of Ernest Hemingway. Hells bells, I had even read one of his books.

My professor had opened my bleary eyes to the immense significance of human connections. Mr. Flood and Omar Khayyam and Ernest Hemingway and—yes, by Jesus, myself. And he had done this by reading a poem and by discussing it with the class. No fanfare. No apologies. No hesitations. Instead, poise. Passion. Insight. Compassion.

Then around mid-semester, after I had written a couple of papers that my professor apparently approved of (he gave me scores of B and A minus), I was on my way out of the classroom when he stopped me and asked me to stay a few minutes; he had something to give me. I was surprised and confused.

We waited until the room had cleared, then Professor Wyrick—that was his name, Professor Green D. Wyrick—handed me a paperback with a brightly-colored cover. *The Grass Harp* by Truman Capote. On the back was a picture of a young man—impossibly young for a novelist, I thought—lying on a couch looking youthfully bright-eyed and winsome.

"I think you might like this book," Professor Wyrick said. "Keep it. And let me know what you think of it."

That was all he said. I thanked him and shook his hand. I felt awkward and grateful, confused and anxious. I could not imagine why he had chosen me to receive the book.

And to this day his reasons, whatever they might have been, remain a mystery. Professor Wyrick is dead now, having spent much of his life teaching with considerable dignity, then having suffered the indignity of an alcoholic's demise. He was my professor in any number of classes, including the writing of fiction. I met regularly with him as he supervised my master's thesis, a novel (unpublished), and we spent many evenings together sipping cold beer and talking about whatever might have been on our minds.

He taught me to respect, but never to worship, the written word. He taught me that all of us, in one way or another, are connected. He taught me, perhaps without knowing the extent to which the lesson took, the value of lyricism in the writing of prose.

The Grass Harp by Truman Capote. "I think you might like this book. Keep it. And let me know what you think of it."

I think it's one hell of a gift, Professor Wyrick. I still have it. It does what maybe you intended it to do. Like the wind through the Indian grass in the novel, its influence continues to sing.

William Kloefkorn lives in Lincoln, Neb., and enjoys spending time with his wife, children, and grandchildren. He has authored several collections of poetry as well as a collection of short stories and four memoirs. Professor Emeritus of English at Nebraska Wesleyan, Kloefkorn was named the Nebraska State Poet in 1982.

Acknowledgments

FOR THEIR LOVE, INTELLIGENCE, and positive influence, I would like to thank all of the formal teachers in my life, in particular, elementary: Sister Francis Louise, Mrs. Maskers, Miss McVeigh, Sister Mary Ruth, Miss Marge Hansen; high school: Brother David, Brother William, Mrs. Dyer, Mr. Gubbels, Senorita Burgos, Mr. Hoy; college: Anastasia Herin, Brother Vincent; graduate school: Dr. John Hill, Dr. Joanne Carlson,

Dr. James Schaffer, and my cooperating teacher and mentor, Barb Howe.

I would also like to thank my large and loving Irish-American family whom I love very much: Mom Mary Agnes, Roger, Cindy, Laurel, Joe, Charlie, Ali, Robbie, Adam, Ben, Kevin, Mary Jo, Julie, Tim, Ryan, Abby, Chris, Kip, Aiden, Andie, Katie, Jan, Brian, Loni, Jim, Dianne, Mike, Becca, Matt, Jason, Jerry, Colleen, Peter, Dan, Tyler, and Tanner.

Huge thanks to my surrogate kids whom I love like my own: Billy, Rachelle, Cartney, Ciaran, Ryan, Kay, Harry, Josie, Jacqui, Julia, Matthew, Christine, Lennon, Jonathan, and Isabella.

I also thank and am so proud of my former students, many of whom are now teachers, principals, firefighters, police officers, singers, actors, corporate leaders, business owners, photographers, professional athletes, and great contributors to society. It was an honor to be a part of your lives.

Thanks to my favorite music man Allen and his wife, Betty. Thanks to my trainer Mark and his beautiful wife, Julie and their son, Markus.

Thanks to my dearest life-long friend and teacher Lydia; all my favorite teacher colleagues and friends, especially Jan and Rob, Rosie and Chuck, Daryl and Shirley, Bob B., Jody and Denny, Tim and Shelli, Jim and Beth, Martha and Bob, Jack and Becky, Todd, and Marilyn B., who provided early editing.

Thanks to my summer school teaching friends at Boys Town High School; to my teacher friends at Beverly Hills Prep School, especially Violet, Joon, and Chris; to my Nebraska Scholars Institute gifted summer school teacher friends, especially Bill, Jim, Randy, Oscar, Jan, Linda, Jane, Greg, John, Connie, Anne, Carolyn and the multi-talented musical Gulizia Brothers (Tony and Joey). Thanks to godmother Colleen, Dan, Martin, Glen and Debbie, Kate, Maggie, Jeff, Lynn, Nick, Kyle, Hannah, Jay, Val, Piper, Taylor, and Christine.

Thanks to all my 139 first and second cousins, and a special thanks to Cuz Gail for the laughs and listening ear, to Steve and Tammy for a lifetime of brownies, to Jan for haircuts, hair colors, and shaved heads. Thanks to my favorite godmother and aunt, Alice.

Thanks to my current team at work: Amy, Marquita, Stephanie, and Brian, and to my extended team, Rose, Joni, Jana, Jean, Suzanne, John, Kevin, Carol, Rhonda, Nicole, Sandra, and Doris.

Thanks to my publishers, designers, editors, and marketers at Concierge Marketing, Inc., especially Lisa, Ellie, Gary, Erin, and Sandra. Thanks also to my lawyer, Denny, and my accountant, Melodie.

And last, but certainly not least, I would like to thank the contributors of the chapters in this book and the teachers who influenced them so positively. I enjoyed meeting all of you, talking to you, and discussing an extremely important topic: *Who is one of your favorite teachers?*

Oh, and thank you, dear reader. Now go thank a teacher!

About John Morrissey

FOR THE LAST THIRTY-SIX years, John Morrissey has been a teacher.

For most of those years, he taught English, Public Speaking, and Special Education at the same Midwestern high school. For all of those years, he taught summer school, night school, and weekend college to supplement his income. For one of those years, he left the Midwest to be the Dean of Students at Beverly Hills Prep School, only longing to return to the Midwest. For the past ten years, he has taught leadership classes for Corporate America's Fortune 500 companies.

John holds a BA degree in English, Speech, and Drama, and an MS degree in Special Education (Learning Disabilities). During his twenty-year tenure at Ralston High School in Omaha, Neb., he was the Freshman Basketball Coach, Student Council Sponsor, Prom Sponsor, Academic Decathlon Coach, and Junior Class Sponsor. He has been on the adjunct faculty at Metropolitan Community College, University of Nebraska, College of St. Mary, and Drake University.

He taught summer school at Boys Town High School. He has travelled the country as a Leadership Trainer for Fortune 500 companies. He is a member of National Speakers Association and American Society for Training and Development.

John is currently President of John Morrissey International, a speaking and consulting business.

His awards include Nebraska Teacher of the Year Finalist, Nebraska State Outstanding Student Council Sponsor, Phi Delta Kappa Showcase

Teacher, University of Nebraska Distinguished Alumni Award, Christa McAuliffe Excellence in Teaching Award, and *Omaha World-Herald* Distinguished Teacher Award.

John is also an avid Wish Granter and Speaker for the Make-A-Wish Foundation.

Finally, John believes thanking a teacher is something we all should continue to do.

To know even one life has breathed easier
because you have lived, this is to have succeeded.

—R. W. Emerson

John Morrissey Presents!

ADMIT IT. IT'S A little scary to hire a speaker for an event. Every group requires and deserves something special just for them—when you are planning the event, you deserve to get the very best presentation for your dollar. Plus, your audience wants an entertaining, informative experience; after all, they are devoting their time, attention and possibly money to attend your event.

John Morrissey spent decades perfecting his presentations and his speaking skills, as well as three decades as a teacher and corporate trainer. He knows your audience and he knows the not-so-ordinary secrets to reaching the hearts of every one of the people attending. His goal is to inspire people to think, act, or be just a bit different from when they arrived. Because even one change creates the opportunity for people—and organizations—to go from ordinary to extraordinary.

Want to chat about how John can help you create a not-so-ordinary experience for your group of teachers, administrators, parents, students or co-workers? Email John at jmorrissey2@cox.net.